MW00764305

Also by Bob Hocking...

A Parkside View

Volumes 1 & 2

Bob Hocking

First published in 2018 by
Parkside – Backpack Productions

Some material and content versions released previously –
2003-2017

www.inmybackpack.com

Hocking, Bob
A Parkside View
Volumes 1 & 2

ISBN-13: 978-1986104401

ISBN-10: 1986104400

Set in Times New Roman

Cover photograph by Terry Hocking

Cover design by Bob Hocking

In My Backpack logo (also known as "The Gus Logo")
designed by Jay Gillen
© Parkside – Backpack Productions

This book is dedicated to Cathy and Barbara. They know the deeper reasons for this. I thank them both for their support and friendship. For this part...

It is always possible for you to make a difference. You may never know how timely or meaningful your actions are, so when offered a choice... be positive and kind.

Table of Contents

Introduction

A *Parkside View* was first released as a newsletter in July of 2016. By the end of 2017, eighteen consecutive issues had been finished and distributed.

Containing a combination of original material and content drawn from my writing archives, each issue has presented at least two essays, along with occasional spotlights pointed in assorted directions.

With Volume 1 wrapped up and Volume 2 set in motion, it became evident that by the end of 2017 I was going to have a decent number of pieces presented in the newsletter. The final total for Volumes 1 and 2 reached forty-three essays... eighteen originals and twenty-five From the Backpack. This collection contains all of those essays (along with two more included as a foreword and an afterword). The originals from the newsletter have only appeared on those pages previously.

A Parkside View

Several years ago—decades, actually—I described myself as an observer of life.

To be fair, it wasn't a fully accurate description.

The idea behind the thought was an attempt to create a kind of classic smell-the-roses scenario. Someone appreciating things as they moved along. Picture a bench in a park being used as a viewing platform and you get the idea.

Time moves along. And every so often, that observer of life concept brings about a potentially different perspective… one of observation and not involvement. And that possibility is the one that scares me.

Years ago, I had a friend that used to joke about black licorice. He loved it. No… let's stress that… he *loved* black licorice. One of his small pleasures in life came from telling his children that they hated it. More for him. And, since there are a fair number of people that don't like black licorice—we're not talking about chocolate—his black licorice master plan worked for many years. Their father was weird, one of those crazy people that liked black licorice, and the kids just rolled with it.

The weird twist of the story, and the connection to my bench in the park, is that the kids never tried black licorice. It is something one might consider natural. A moment where you really will never know unless you try it is placed into action. But, for them, the situation just felt perfectly resolved. That's dad... he's telling us we don't like it... he would know.

In the case of licorice hoarding, it's a funny story. In the case of isolating yourself from parts of life, to the extent of perhaps even passing judgment when you don't have the knowledge to truly understand, it turns instead into a cautionary tale.

A few days ago, I heard a story about a couple that invested all of their money into a boat. Literally. Quit their jobs, sold most of their belongings, bought a sailboat and planned on the possibility of circling the globe. Didn't work out too well. In an unfamiliar area, they struck something and the boat sank. A total loss on the second day of travel. And you'd almost want to feel very bad for them... as friends or family, you would feel bad for them... until...

This couple effectively invested their future into a sailboat, even though they had no experience sailing a boat. I don't want to be cruel, because they lost a great deal, but in reading the story I kept thinking about how fortunate they were. Their boat sank close to land. Given their knowledge and experience, this was a disaster waiting to happen. And for their sake, and their dog, it was a good thing the worst took place where and when it did, instead of hundreds of miles away from land during a storm they were most certainly unprepared to face.

I broke my ankle a few years ago. Really broke it. Screws and plates and other hardware broke it.

During some physical therapy, I spent a session with someone that really needed a good smack. I was attempting all of the exercises and stretches and work. One piece of equipment was a round, inflated step. Think of half a ball, two-feet wide and about a foot high. Heavy-duty rubber and filled with air. I believe it's called a balance ball trainer, with the idea being to improve coordination, strength and, yes, balance.

The suggestion presented to me was that I should stand to one side of the ball, jump up and toward the ball, land on my bad ankle, step to switch and land on my good ankle, then push off to land on the other side of the ball. Next, reverse my motion to head the other way. Side to side. Repeat. Forty-eight years old, out of shape, over a dozen screws in my ankle, I immediately responded vocally with a "oh hell no" as visions of my ankle snapping danced in my head.

There is an art to claiming a spot on that bench in the park. There is an art to claiming a position observing the world. You need to have a recognition and respect for your own abilities and experiences. You need to understand when to jump in, and when to stand still. You don't need to burn your hand to know that touching the hot stove is a bad idea (but it helps to have a concept of what would happen if you did).

I don't like black licorice. I have tried it.

The other day I ordered a balance ball trainer step thingy of my own. I will use it. I can't say that I'll ever progress to jumping side to side, but I haven't given up on the idea.

You can't sit out every dance.

For now, I'm headed over to the park. I've got a paper to read, and a bit of time to invest in just watching the world go by.

Fireflies and chipmunks

I was on the deck a few nights ago, and the fireflies were simply amazing. It was a brilliant, wonderful evening. Clear skies... temperature just right... and the dancing of lights spread out from the edge of the brush across the yard. Back in early April, I broke my ankle. The recovery has been long, difficult and painful. But one of the most haunting parts of the process is quite likely something you wouldn't expect.

For more than a year... almost sixteen months, in fact... I had been heading into our backyard each night. It was a way, for me, to offer my respect after the loss of our beloved pets. Since 1993, I had ended every day at home by taking the dogs out one last time before bed. That continued all the way to January of 2015.

It didn't seem right ending the day without a visit to the yard. It was my way of tucking them in. As time moved along, and I continued to head outside, it became more. I shared my thoughts with them, and said goodnight. It also became a peaceful moment of opportunity to bring the day to a close. Part meditative... part this and that... it was a nice way to place a ribbon on the gift of today.

(And yes, I fully understand how sappy "place a ribbon on the gift of today" sounds.)

That moment was stolen from me in the time it took to fall to the ground. For days I simply wasn't physically able to cover the distance, and for weeks I couldn't navigate the path. For more than two months I couldn't get outside.

And then that changed...

Gaining strength and mobility, little by little, I was able to not only think about heading into the yard as the sun set and the stars appeared... I was able to do it.

When the tradition of steeping outside began for me, I was handed a treasure I wasn't expecting. The wind bringing life to the trees... the noises being shared from surrounding woods... shooting stars cascading above... all wonderful and amazing.

On a June evening, spending a few moments in the yard to finish off a beautiful summer day, the fireflies swirled and performed.

The following morning, I went out onto the deck with a cup of coffee. As I sat there for a bit, the birds eventually adjusted to my presence and came to the feeders. A pair of chipmunks appeared... chased each other... and gathered some of the seed that had fallen to the ground.

(Sappy ribbons all over the place at this point.)

Not too bad a thing to sit back and take it all in, no matter the impulse and motivation responsible for doing so. In fact, it's pretty special. And it's nice to have that back.

Just don't inconvenience me

I don't like people.

Maybe that seems a bit strong.

But I didn't say I *hate* people... just a current state of *serious* dislike. It's a step or two above that sentiment of "if all these people would just leave me alone, I could get my work done" in a situation where, naturally, those same people I wish would leave me alone are exactly why I have work... and a job... in the first place.

A friend of mine had a great thought about dealing with the hassles associated with life... both on personal and professional levels. Her saying?

"Don't inconvenience me."

Essentially you could take that expression and place anything you want in front of it. Kids want to have a sleepover on Friday night? Fine, just don't inconvenience me. Going to be late for work? Fine, as long as it doesn't inconvenience me. And so on and on. I don't want to spend Friday night driving around to pick up kids and Saturday bringing them back home. I don't want to spend the majority of my shift cleaning up things you should have handled.

It's not quite a state of burnout, when the task itself just seems frustrating and people are interrupting you. It's different. Beyond that. It's the person in the express lane at the grocery store... trying to get away with five items too many, and they also forgot to bring cash or a debit card, and they can't seem to find their checkbook, and oh if you'll just give them a minute. It's the person weaving over the lines on the road, doing ten miles an hour under the speed limit for over five miles of road where you can't pass, and then lowering the cell phone out of view when they pass the police officer parked on the side of the road.

My stepson has a great idea for cell phone users. If you have a cell phone in your car, you should be required to display the phone number on the back of your car. That way, when you start driving stupidly, the person you are blocking can call you up, have you put the other person on hold, and tell you to hang up, pay attention and drive. I admit, it still needs some work, but it does have several great points in its favor.

When I was growing up I used to hear people say—and I'm sure all of you heard this as well—either "there's no such thing as a stupid question" or "the only stupid question is the one you don't ask." Well, they were wrong. There are *plenty* of stupid questions. Lots and lots and lots of them.

And people aren't afraid to ask them.

And inconvenience me.

I suppose this whole inconvenience things leads into a more important question: What constitutes an inconvenience? If I don't want you to inconvenience me, then I'm saying there are some things that I would not be upset by. Things I wouldn't say were an inconvenience if presented with them. Perhaps, just perhaps, there are things I might be interested in. Which of course, leads us to what might be the more appropriate form of "don't inconvenience me." A simple question...

"What's in it for me?"

Ah, yes. Now that's better. I'll take care of this for you, but... what's in it for me? No, I don't mind doing that, but... what's in it for me? So, instead of being put out by the whole darn thing... why do I want to do it?... what's my motivation?

I used to know this guy... tremendous ability to socialize. You could introduce him to anyone, and from the first words out of his mouth he would engage them with a great conversation. The funny thing was, I also noticed something else about him. You could put him in a room with... oh pick a number... 10... 20... 30 people that he didn't know. And within thirty minutes not only could he point to the majority of the room and correctly identify them by name and occupation, but he could also tell you what all of those people he named could do for him...

> *"He works for an electronics company and he's going to get me some great speakers for my car. She works for a record store and knows how to order that CD I've wanted but haven't been able to find. And remember how I was hoping to get engaged? Well, she makes custom jewelry settings and is going to design the ring with me. And he works for a travel company, heard me talking about it, and is going to send me information on special deals for magical proposal settings."*

...and so on. He was, and is, good. Give him five minutes with a person and not only will he know their name and family history, he'll also have them contracted to build a deck in his backyard.

Strange thing is, I don't *ever* recall seeing him in anyone else's backyard building their deck. Know what I mean?

I got married just over six years ago. One of the best and smartest things I ever did in my life. Along with a wonderful bride, I gained two stepsons. And quite quickly, I learned something very valuable. If you don't hide the leftovers, they'll be gone by morning. Interpret that in any way you see fit, simply understand that sometimes it isn't such a bad thing to keep things from the kids. To be greedy. Unfortunately, the youngest one is on to us, and he's also taller than us now. Hiding things is more difficult than ever.

But the thing is, like it or not, society in general is designed around two concepts. First, an equal exchange where I'll take care of this for you as long as we can finish off that for me. Or second, look out for number one. I'm sorry about this folks, but let's face it, in society today it is virtually accepted as being better to receive instead of to give.

I worked with someone several years ago and we were exchanging horror stories about social lives. (Ok, we were talking about my horrible social life.) His summation of the dating world?

> *"If you don't reach into the jar, you ain't getting a cookie."*

A smart man.

And maybe that's the real summation to it all. See, we grow up and go from dreaming about our future to actually having to pay the bills during our present. Instead of becoming a professional athlete, a famous musician, or maybe even a fireman, we end up having to pay rent, buy a car, and support a family. And we take what we need to in order to pay those bills. Dreams have a price. And so does life.

Far too many of us wind up looking at the work as an inconvenience as a result. It's not what we want to be doing. It's not what we would be doing if we had a choice. It's what we have to be doing. So stop bothering me, stop interrupting me, stop inconveniencing me.

Unless, of course, it's in my best interest to listen to what you have to say.

Would you rather... an old lesson on doubling

I seem to recall the first time I saw some version of this question, I was in first grade. (But... not completely sure about that.) Here we go...
Which would you select?
Option A – $1,000,000
Option B – It's September 1st. You have a penny. Tomorrow that amount will double, and you have two-cents. It continues that way for the entire month, each day the amount of the previous day being doubled. You get the amount for the day after the doubling on September 30th.
So... $1,000,000, or, the total on the final day of a penny doubled every day for a month?
(And now we get to do the math.)

Day	Total	Day	Total
1	$0.01	16	$327.68
2	$0.02	17	$655.36
3	$0.04	18	$1,310.72

4	$0.08	19	$2,621.44
5	$0.16	20	$5,242.88
6	$0.32	21	$10,485.76
7	$0.64	22	$20,971.52
8	$1.28	23	$41,943.04
9	$2.56	24	$83,886.08
10	$5.12	25	$167,772.16
11	$10.24	26	$335,544.32
12	$20.48	27	$671,088.64
13	$40.96	28	$1,342,177.28
14	$81.92	29	$2,684,354.56
15	$163.84	30	$5,368,709.12

Yeah... you knew there was a trick, but perhaps you didn't realize it would be that big of a trick.

The end result is so striking, it seems almost impossible to think there was even a choice to consider.

But... check out the chart... even around the middle of the month there doesn't appear to be any way someone selecting one million dollars is going to have any regrets. Heck, two-thirds of the way through the month the penny has just made its way past five thousand dollars.

I've been thinking about this lesson for a variety of reasons in recent years. Most notably when it comes to business. Because as I am asked to pay additional fees... navigate automated telephone systems... and tolerate poor customer service, if not poor product quality as well... I keep wondering how these companies are surviving. Because they most certainly aren't doing anything to earn my long-term or repeat business.

(The general implication being treat me poorly, and today I leave... treat all the customers poorly, and tomorrow someone else leaves, the next day a couple more leave, and the next day...)

There are all sorts of similar stories or thoughts available… the long journeys that begin by taking the first step… worry about the quality and the reward will take care of itself… and so on.

Unfortunately, I don't know how many people recognize the craziness swirling around.

For example… how are your retirement savings being handled right now? I would be willing to wager that almost all of the answers fall into one of three thoughts…

> Number one – Retirement? Ha! I don't have anything left after paying my bills to invest in retirement.

> Number two – I have a guy for that. (In this case meaning the person is putting something aside, but really has absolutely no clue where the monies are.)

> Number three – I have a guy for that. (In this case meaning that the person actually is "the guy" and they know darn well how and where their monies have been invested, or, the person recognizes their own weaknesses when it comes to handling retirement savings and has wisely taken the time to find a truly qualified professional to handle things.)

Here's the fun part… I believe the third group is by _far_ the smallest group.

Most reputable sources estimate that as of today at least one-third of working age Americans have a grand total of zero dollars saved for retirement.

Let's pause for a moment.

(Ok… I will repeat that.)

Most reputable sources estimate that as of today at least one-third of working age Americans have a grand total of zero dollars saved for retirement.

And, actually, it's worse than that. Many of those sources say that's too conservative and place the number above forty-percent for their figures. As if that wasn't bad enough, they usually continue... of those people saving anything for retirement, they believe that more than ninety-percent are dramatically short of where they should be when it comes to retirement savings.

I never intended for this essay to be a lesson about pennies, better business practices, or 401K plans. Instead, it's more of sounding a bit of an alarm.

A few months ago, I was out looking at computers. And for those of us in the middle-of-the-road mainstream, that meant a decently-priced unit running some current version of a Microsoft operating system. Funny thing, you can no longer get Word and Excel and Outlook and PowerPoint (and more) when buying a brand spanking new computer. You have to purchase that software separately.

Amazing thing about the software. There are choices to be made. And those choices go beyond making a decision about whether or not you need Outlook. Lots of decisions... here are just two...

One or more PCs? A one-year service subscription or permanent software installation?

It goes on. There are all sorts of packages for home and business and students and more.

One of the real head-scratchers for me is that one-year subscription. About the only way it makes sense is if you know you'll only have that computer for less than fifty-two weeks. Which, I suppose is possible, but for most of us... well... I just don't see many of us buying a computer that is going to be completely useless and out of our lives just one year after setting up Word.

As a whole, we're simply not making smart decisions.

And that is what this essay is supposed to be about.

In many grocery stores right now, you can buy a gallon of drinking water for a dollar. Walk into any convenience store in the country, and chances are pretty good a 16-ounce bottle of water will cost you a dollar plus some change. And in both cases, we almost all would certainly pay that amount without a second thought. Point here being... I get it... supply and demand... consider the circumstances.

But what about when given the second thought? What about decisions with no limitations from time and circumstance?

One million dollars is a pretty sweet result, even if the facts outlined at the end ultimately show that a person made a big mistake by picking door number one.

Trouble is... we don't always find such a sweet result at the end.

Everything's coming up pumpkins

The pumpkin craze.

It seems to be worse this year.

It's everywhere. In fact, no, it's more than everywhere. It's completely unavoidable and inescapable. Have you ever seen a room coated in baby powder? And I don't mean spilled the container, baby power is on the carpet, and you have to get the vacuum cleaner for it. I mean clouds of baby powder in the air, settling on every surface, and no matter how much you clean you'll still move something five months later and find baby powder.

That's the pumpkin tidal wave that begins in August in preparation to sweep us under. I guarantee you there have been or will be packages of coffee and cake mix purchased that seem so perfect... only to be less than perfect when discovered on a shelf next April.

Seriously... have you been in a Dunkin Donuts? Within three miles of my home, there are multiple Dunkin Donuts locations. (You probably have a few as well.) There are also several other coffee shops nearby. From all of these java huts, as I sit here in early November to write this, a partial list of available pumpkin items includes...

Pumpkin coffee
Pumpkin hot chocolate
Pumpkin latte
Pumpkin smoothies
Pumpkin bread
Pumpkin donuts
Pumpkin muffins
Pumpkin cookies
Pumpkin whipped cream

Yes. That's right. Pumpkin whipped cream.

We can stop checking off items right there. This is, as I mentioned, a *partial* list. And pumpkin whipped cream is a good place to pause, allow for perspective, and move along. Amazingly though... and I actually took a drive this morning and looked around while I was out... as of yet, no sightings of pumpkin juice. (But fear not Harry Potter fans. One day, of course, at a store near you and me and all of us, there will be. There will be.)

It is still pretty pumpkin crazy.

(Hold on. Side note. Need a disclaimer and points for the everything-pumpkin-loving-side. What is not crazy are pumpkin whoopie pies... Arremony's Quality Bakery... jaw-droppingly awesome from a jaw-droppingly brilliant bakery. We will *not* be making fun of the pumpkin whoopie pies.)

What isn't hard to see in this pumpkin craze is that fall themes and decorations are now at a level that rivals any of the seasons or holidays. You are as likely to see inflatable ghosts in October or inflatable cornucopias in November as you are to see an inflatable Santa in December. By no means am I suggesting that these holidays have overtaken (or can even approach) Christmas in terms of scope, hype, hysteria or monetary measures. But it's only a matter of time before inflatable babies with top hats show up for New Year's Eve. When reaching a point where Christmas overload is a real thing, somehow managing to get the public inflating giant turkeys on lawns while stringing up witch-themed exterior lights around windows are nice touches by those looking to exploit our mass consumerism in a new way.

Hey... I'm not complaining. (And I probably should try to copyright that inflatable New Year's baby idea.) I bought gingerbread Twix to try them. (They were ok. And honestly, barely ok. (And more honestly, not at all great and I wouldn't miss them if I never had them again.)) I was in a Red Robin and tried a gingerbread shake. (That was AWESOME! Highly recommended.) And I will soon have a forest of decorated trees filled with inflatable penguins and such around my front yard to celebrate the impending arrival of the big guy in the red suit.

I enjoy the seasons... like the celebrations... love many of the decorations... cherish the traditions... and participate in the consumerism craze. All year round.

The thing is... this year... the pumpkin is sweeping me up and tossing me around and leaving me dazed.

Pumpkin... pumpkin... pumpkin... pumpkin...

There has been pumpkin in the candy bars, and pumpkin in spreads for crackers, and pumpkin dishes for your holiday tables. Appetizers and meals and desserts and snacks, while at the same time filling the container in your car's cup holder as you make the rounds of holiday errands to get the pumpkin-themed decorations for the pumpkin-season holiday events.

The Great Pumpkin became a part of *Peanuts* legend more than fifty years ago. And these days, Linus doesn't have to wait for an appearance because the great pumpkin is everywhere!

People are buying the lattes and muffins though. (Many of them are likely quite delicious. I suspect many more are not. Why is that a problem? Well... it's not. Instead... I wonder why so many people seem oblivious to what's happening.)

I have found that many of those same people that cry and kick and scream in terror mixed with fear mixed with disgust when Santa makes his first appearance over Labor Day weekend tend to create a very large portion of the people purchasing an inflatable Frankenstein. One man's sleigh bells are another man's jack-o-lanterns.

At some point, someone is going to think about marketing something new and different, swerve away from pumpkins, and we'll suddenly see more gingerbread than ever. This will be followed a few years later by a retro-nouveau campaign for apples. Eventually, pumpkins and gingerbread and apples will all be available as inflatables for your yard. (With overnight shipping. (Free shipping if you order all three.))

The reality though... Linus is probably right: "There are three things I have learned never to discuss with people: religion, politics, and the Great Pumpkin." (And I'm craving whoopie pie.)

Making the most of my two minutes

Her mother walked over to the microwave and set the timer.

Two minutes.

She had two minutes.

When the alarm sounded, that would be it... bed time.

Before her mother's finger even hit the button to start the count, she was gone.

Her first stop was in the family room, where she immediately hopped on the "spinny" chair that had become a favorite during her visit. Unfortunately, with her twin sister and younger brother already in their bedrooms, there was no one to actually spin it, so she had to entertain herself by rocking instead.

Her bedtime countdown tour went into the kitchen to look for some great snack or drink that might have appeared in the twenty-two seconds since she was last looking. Countertops were explored, relatives were kissed, but no chocolate was found.

Then it was off to the living room, where she saw her favorite stuffed animal and decided he needed to have his clothes changed. (Build-A-Bear may be one of the most underappreciated business ideas in years.)

A round of approval was gathered from on-lookers for the Halloween costume that had been packed but was now making a mid-November appearance.

From there she stopped by the open door of the bathroom to explain to her aunt that she had two whole minutes before bed time. If her aunt understood her it would have been amazing, but she was already heading down the hall to see her grandfather.

"I've got two minutes," she said.

"What?" asked Grampa.

"Two minutes. I've got two minutes," she responded, with a bit of frustration.

"I don't understand. Two minutes until what?"

"Two minutes," she explained, taking a deep breath and obviously a bit flustered that Grampa, instead of sharing her excitement, was slowing her down. "Mom set the alarm, and when…"

*Beep * beep * beep*

The alarm was followed by a head turning to the kitchen, wearing the saddest face of sorrow one could imagine.

Her two minutes were up.

My niece was visiting from Australia a few months ago, and this is an outline of the events from the final evening of their trip that led her way to bed. But as she trudged off to goodnight, I found myself laughing. She had managed to pack more into her two minutes than any two minutes of my day. In fact... given two minutes until bed... I would have been trying to figure out if a visit to the bathroom counted against the clock while heading off to put on my pajamas and just get under the sheets. I definitely wouldn't be racing around to make use of every second.

When did that end for me?

I can't remember.

But far too rarely do I make use of time the way I could... or did.

It used to be that I... like all kids... just kept moving until my batteries were shot. Constantly moving... constantly on. These days... well... it seems the most generous to say that I pace myself.

I suppose that isn't a bad thing. It gets me through the day and accomplishes almost everything I set out for my schedule. But it definitely isn't as exciting. It isn't a maximum-value return on every investment.

Tigg and I are working on a deck for our house. Yesterday we cleaned the garage out (had to, we're going to be bolting a support board in behind my work bench). And we did that because the back of the house was still a bit damp (we are painting the garage before the deck gets built). We got a lot done.

And it darn near killed us.

I suppose I won't be running around with a microwave counting down to my bedtime. And I probably won't be thrilled by leaping into every second of every day. But there's a lesson in here... I think... about appreciating the time I have.

Maybe in a few weeks... on a quiet summer evening... sitting on my deck drinking lemonade while the sun is going down... I'll figure out exactly what that lesson is.

A glimpse of the heavens

Did you watch… or make any attempt to watch… the Perseids meteor shower in August?

It's an annual thing, and the 2016 event was expected to be one of the best ever, with some viewers being treated to as many as 150-200 visible streaks of light crossing the sky each hour.

I tried to watch a bit of it, and found myself on a couple of nights sitting on the deck, looking into the night. The lights were out and I was surrounded by beautiful, quiet evenings. And I did see several meteors dance along. Spectacular sights.

I also found myself staring off at the stars, giving a bit of thought to my place in the universe.

Many people with strong religious beliefs look at us, our planet, the universe and all within through the concept of intelligent design. Too complex for chance… perfect for a divine creator.

Gazing off into infinity, such a view seems perfect for the idea of our not being alone. (Indulge me for a moment.)

How often do you do something once?

There are plenty of things that you hope to only do once. Building a deck or a shed... making some significant repair... ok.

But if you find a recipe beyond delicious... you try to make it again. If you can do home repairs as needed, some that need to be done again and again... you do.

While I admit it's a bit of a stretch, if you were able to create stars and galaxies... raise mountains and fill seas and give life... I'm not so certain that you would limit things to our planet.

In between bright and spectacular flashes, I often began wondering about what might be looking back toward me.

Is there... our there... somewhere... beings of some sort wondering about their places in the swirling cosmos?

We get told and taught and shown ways to approach certain moments or activities from outside the box. The intent of such encouragement is to change perspectives and challenge the norms. Simply put, to see things differently.

Just on our planet, we have seen how spinning around, orbiting the sun, views can change based on time and place. A tilted axis provides much of the influences that create seasons while changing the number of daylight hours throughout the year.

How would that change on Mars? Further from the sun? A new viewing stage.

How would that change from outside our solar system... outside our galaxy... from thousands of other places in the universe?

Would Earth even be visible?

We learn things, most of which we forget, about the travels of light and such across distance. It takes more than eight minutes for the light from the Sun to reach Earth. Many of the stars we see in the evening may actually be gone... not there... as we get to enjoy their presence in the night sky.

On a perfect summer evening, with clear skies and beautiful temperatures and the Perseids overhead, the universe itself appears for the show.

A round of Tomato Juice

Over the past few days, we've been gathering as friends and family and exchanging stories about Ellen. Should be no surprise in that. We all cared tremendously for her. We all shared moments with her. Whether they bring smiles and laughs, or crying and tears, it is how strong our experiences have been, and how we feel about Ellen, that creates such wonderful memories. It helps to remember.

I've been telling many stories about Ellen. Terry and I have recalled them over hundreds and hundreds of miles of driving. We've shared them with Richard, and family, and friends. We've shared them in the car, as general exchanges during the afternoon, and over dinner. There's one story I haven't told though. And I'd like to tell it now…

Almost all of us can picture a delightful, amazing, and bordering upon sinfully good indulgence. Perhaps it's warm chocolate chip cookies or a beyond description sundae. Something that just tempts you as the most incredible and often unsatisfied craving.

During two decades, I have been fortunate to share many moments with Ellen. Terry and I have been on several adventures with her and Richard. And when it comes to indulgences for her, I can tell you Ellen loved good wine and enjoyed good food. She was passionate about travel, and thrilled by the opportunities to host friends at her home. But there is one thing that, just by seeing it on a menu, could cause her to enter a state of dazed bliss, with her eyes glazed over as a visible state of euphoria overtook her.

Tomato juice.

I know. Terry and I never understood the appeal of tomato juice either. But we witnessed it appeal to Ellen on multiple occasions.

I think part of the beauty of tomato juice for Ellen was that when found it was almost always an unexpected and unpredicted treat. We'd wander into a restaurant for breakfast, normally with plans for a long and wondrous day ahead. She'd pick up a menu, and, if you were watching her, you'd pretty much be able to pinpoint the very moment she spotted it… there would be a light pause in her speech if she was speaking, or she'd suddenly wiggle in her seat. Subtle for certain, but noticeable if you were watching.

You sit down in a restaurant and a server takes your beverage order. How long does it take to complete the delivery of drinks to a table? One minute? Four? Whatever. Generally it's not too long. But for Ellen, the time from speaking "tomato juice" to having it placed in front of her appeared to be a torturous pleasure that lasted an eternity. To say she'd fidget and squirm, unable to sit still would be a significant understatement. But even more than that body language of exquisite anticipation, the expression on her face was priceless. It would best be described as a combination of her personal conviction that the greatest treat in the world was on its way, united with a glowing satisfaction of having made a tremendous selection that was going to work out wonderfully, topped off with a "ha, ha, I have tomato juice and you don't" whipped cream and cherry on top smugness.

A few years ago I heard someone discussing the concept of personal losses and death. And they conveyed an observation that I have carried with me ever since. I just like it. I find a sense of comfort within it.

The idea was founded on the expression passed on, and what might be understood as an almost literal reading of the phrase. The people that we meet leave an impression upon us. It's the experiences we share and the memories we create together... it's their approach to anything and everything, and the lessons we learn by the way they act and carry themselves. And, in death, they don't truly leave us... instead... they have been *passed on* to us.

It's those amazing vacations, and the smiles we have recalling them. It's the recipes we've tried, and will try again and again. It's the values and traditions and tiny little things that filled parts of ourselves, and make us the individuals we are today and will be tomorrow.

Yes, an amazing person has departed. Their legacy though... the care of that legacy has been passed on to us.

Each and every day from now on, I will miss Ellen. But there is something I hope she has passed on to me... something I hope to pass on to you...

Tomato juice.

Don't worry... this isn't a literal wish... you won't need to break out some pepper, a stalk of celery, or even hope there's some vodka around.

Instead... my wish is that at least once every day, you have a tomato juice moment of your own. A moment so special that you find yourself wiggling in your seat, eyes in an unfocused haze of bliss, wrapped in a blanket of anticipation and satisfaction... a moment of pure joy and tranquility.

There is nothing in life that is guaranteed to any of us. And while we all need to be mindful of our actions and prepare for the future, I'd say it's equally important to take some time every day and indulge in the present.

Enjoy.

Are your contacts up to date?

When was the last time you checked your Christmas card list?

(Ok... ok... easy... I know it's September. I also recognize some don't celebrate Christmas, and others don't send cards. Stay with me. This isn't about Christmas. At all. It's the idea of the list.)

I have long contended—and still do believe—that there are three phases involved in sending cards. Initially, we go through our address book or other records, address the envelopes, and send out a wave of greetings and sentiments to friends and family. Often, when we find ourselves with a few remaining cards, we might check our lists twice and decide on a few more to send so we don't have to store the leftovers. And then, when cards begin arriving at our home, we are confronted with how to handle receiving one from a person we didn't include in our original mailings.

Where this essay is headed however has little to do with any of the phases or intentions of card sending. Instead, it's the list itself.

All of us have some form of address book. It might be a physical collection and it could be digitally stored. Some of it will be highly personal and important... parents, siblings, friends, etc. Some of it will be quite functional... doctors or service providers (furnace cleaning, lawn care, and so on). And from that we arrive at two distinctions:

(1) When it comes to the mention of a "Christmas card list" we arrive at a certain level of personal relationships. Most of us are not thinking about sending greeting cards out to our dentists, primary care physicians or home improvement contractors. No need to explore why we would or wouldn't, or make supporting statements of their value in our lives. Of course they are important. It's just the professional relationship that exists, overcoming the informal expressions of the season.

(2) Most of the people that we interact with often have shared some form of contact information with us. We have a phone number, home address, or e-mail details for them. If we needed to get a message to them, in a way that could generate a response in a timely manner, more likely than not we could.

Let's allow virtually everything I've said so far to take a place as a foundation. Because here's the twist...

One of the things I find most frustrating is that I have a handful of people I can't contact. Their phone numbers, mailing addresses, and e-mail accounts have changed. While trying to find them, many of those same pieces of information have changed for me. They don't appear to be using Facebook or Twitter or SnapAGram or whatever the latest is in social media.

On television, some of the recent back-to-school efforts focused on having children prepared. And part of that included experimenting with whether or not kids know emergency information such as how to get home or reach someone if needed. This may come as no surprise... as we navigate a technological age where telephone contacts can be filed or accessed in ways that require little thought or memorization of actual numbers... a pretty sizeable number of kids don't know their home number, or, the cell phone numbers for mom and dad.

Every year, I pull out the information needed to send out our annual letter. And, pretty much without exception, every year I find that updates need to be made. Almost always a pretty basic reason... people moved. Just about every year at least one or two cards get returned with no forwarding information.

A few weeks ago, my sister-in-law called. She told me she had changed her cell phone number. And, of course, life immediately happened, so I haven't updated the number yet. It's a fairly minor thing – I have her home number... can send her e-mails or Facebook messages... her home address is exactly the same... other members of the family know how to reach her. No worries in contacting her. But the fact remains... our records aren't quite right.

A Christmas card list is essentially just label... where more accurately it's a way of referring to our records of people we consider important and/or regularly reach out to. Experience shows that many of us can't immediately remember information without some sort of reminder or reference, don't have all of the details as current as we might like, often have lapses we wish we could fix, and every twelve months or less will find a change has occurred and needs to be updated.

When was the last time you checked your Christmas card list?

Was it Christmas?

A Tale of Two City
Welcome to Savannah
Bob and Terry on Tour 2012, with Ellen and Richard

So you're planning a vacation to Savannah, Georgia. And for this reason or that, you find yourself having a conversation with someone and the subject of the trip comes up. Usually, it happens at some point when you make a very simple statement: "Yeah, we're going to Savannah."

One of two reactions will follow.

"Oh, I've always wanted to go there!"

Or...

"You are going to have an incredible time!"

And that's pretty much it.

It's like some magic spell that Savannah holds over people where only two responses are permissible. Reaction one – someone that hasn't been to Savannah expresses that they have it rated highly on their list for someday. And reaction two – someone that has been to Savannah confirms that it's worthy of a place near the top of everyone's list for someday.

Happens *every* time.

Ok… sure… there might be a person that does not offer one of those responses. I suppose there could be people that don't care at all about heading to Savannah. Just about anything's possible.

The thing is… I've never met one of such people. Not one.

(It's all very mysterious. And recently it became quite apparent to us.)

Terry, Ellen, Richard and I have always wanted to go to Savannah. Plans were put into motion for a visit. But as we mapped out our few days and the vacation crept closer, something occurred to me. All those people that *loved* Savannah? Yeah… umm… they never said *why* they loved it.

Tell someone you're going to San Francisco. You'll hear about the Golden Gate Bridge, Lombard Street, wine country, Muir Woods, and more.

Washington, DC? Smithsonian… Arlington… The White House… pandas at the National Zoo… and more.

New York? Times Square… Empire State Building… Statue of Liberty.

Sydney, Australia? The Opera House… Harbour Bridge.

And always more.

Of course I'm missing some fabulous sites in these cities, but as examples you get the idea. Why wasn't anyone openly sharing the to-do list of Savannah?

Eventually I began asking a second question whenever the subject came up and I had been told I was going to love Savannah. I wanted to know what types of places and things we should be sure to include. And every time I asked these "You are going to have an incredible time!" people what we should do, not one person provided a single suggestion.

Not one person.

Not one suggestion.

Not one.

In fact... crickets. It became a conversation ending question. And the more I tried to get some thoughts, the more it began to rattle around in my mind and concern me.

Once, from a person that seemed a bit confused that I would even ask what to do, I was told that Savannah is just beautiful. (And it is.)

I couldn't get a restaurant recommendation though... or experiences with museums or historical sites... or advice on where to stay... or... well... anything.

And all of this seemed stranger when I learned I wasn't alone. Somewhat jokingly, I mentioned the thought to Terry, Ellen and Richard. Their eyes revealed a bit of shock as we all realized that our experiences were strikingly similar.

We were going to Savannah. We were excited to be going to Savannah. People that had been to Savannah were telling us we should be excited about going to Savannah. But apparently, no one knew why.

So here we are... approaching the Savannah travel diaries and Savannah "Best of..." column... and I'm glad that I took a few months to put things together. It provided some perspective. Because even after the visit, I find at times I'm still a bit confused by Savannah in ways that are difficult to describe.

I have arrived at a conclusion though.

Savannah is two distinct places... and one great place.

There's the tourist Savannah and the historic Savannah. And more so than any other place I have ever been... *any* city, state, or country... there is a divide between the touristy and the historical that is difficult to separate and impossible to unite. Characteristics blur. It's really quite bizarre.

We can start with the tourism.

If you go to Savannah, you will be stunned by the overwhelming presence of two things: Number one... Paula Deen. Number two... *Midnight in the Garden of Good and Evil.* I'm telling you this now. Overwhelming.

You might even tell yourself that you expect a lot of material based on these two... and you can think you have prepared for the onslaught... and you will still be *stunned* by how much they are on display.

They are the driving forces behind the bus tours... the shops... the restaurants... and everything else. They provide tourism and touchstones and connections to virtually every element of life in Savannah. And honestly, nothing else is close. Even when not directly mentioning Paula or the book, you'll get references to The Lady and Sons restaurant and the Bird Girl statue. These culinary and literary giants cast an immense shadow across the region... a shadow of such size and dominance that it is frankly astounding considering the longevity of the city and its place in history.

Of course, they are not the only touristy aspects of the city. The shops... especially along the water... will seem familiar to anyone that has been to San Francisco, Fort Lauderdale, Newport, or another recognizable waterside destination. Obviously the beaches and mansions and histories change... but the concept is the same. Been there... bought the t-shirt.

Down near the Savannah River is East River Street. And strolling along this road you'll come across places to shop and eat. Here's what I wrote about John's Pass Boardwalk after a 2010 visit to Madeira Beach in Florida:

> *Sure... some of the shops were kind of boring. Seemed like the pattern of stores repeated at every fourth door. (Door number one... shells and dolphin statues and discount t-shirts, none of which truly captured the feeling of Madeira Beach but seemed more likely set up to be just cheap enough and just beach-themed enough to take a dollar or two out of your pocket. Door number two... perhaps a restaurant or bar or store selling water. Door number three... something amazing and different and unusual that really attracted you by offering brilliant original stuff, plus the feeling that if you didn't pay attention and look at everything you were definitely missing something. Door number four... shells and dolphin statues and discount t-shirts, none of which truly captured the feeling of Madeira Beach but seemed to be ordered from exactly the same catalogue that was used at door number one (and I mean, exactly the same catalogue). Door number five... perhaps a restaurant or bar or store selling water... and you see how this is beginning to repeat.) The goal was to get to as many door number three locations as possible.*

And in Savannah on East River Street? Same idea... repeating stores... seen them all before... bought the t-shirt.

I mentioned that things blur and overlap and yet don't mix in Savannah though.

We were talking to a waiter in a restaurant on our first night. We had parked our car and planned on spending the after-dinner hours walking around the area and wondered if there were some things we should look for. He talked a bit in generalities... surprise, still no specific advice, "it's all great"... and then he mentioned how much he loved the history of River Street.

According to his lesson for us, not years ago... not decades ago... quite literally *centuries* ago, the ships sailing from Europe into Savannah would come across the ocean and up the Savannah River loaded with ballast stones for stability. They would pick up cargo and leave the ballast stones behind. These stones were in turn used in the construction of buildings... stairs... and, for this waiter's story most specifically, for the actual street of River Street.

River Street is a cobblestone road of sorts – formed from the very history... the very ballast stones... of the city's early days. It is quite impressive and stunning when you are standing on River Street and are aware of this.

Now... let's try to bring these elements together. Touristy like everyplace... unique and amazing historical significance few locations could compare with... literally woven into the fabric of the city.

That's Savannah.

You want touristy? *Midnight in the Garden of Good and Evil* and the Bird Girl are on display in every gift shop, from copies of the book to different sizes of the statue. And suddenly, it blurs, and you are across from Monterey Square... at the Mercer House.

You want touristy? You find The Lady and Sons... cookbooks and Paula Deen bus tours. And then that overlap comes into play... just casually speaking to the owner of The Christmas Shop on Bull Street and she asks if you're in the area for lunch. And when you ask why, she refers you to the greatest restaurant you might ever set foot in – Mrs. Wilkes' Dining Room.

Savannah isn't simply what you experience… it's *how* you experience it. And that realization can create quite a different visit to this gorgeous city.

Visually it is striking.

The people we met were all wonderful.

Unlike those advising us though, I will break the mystery and give you some specifics.

Stop and check out some of the squares and get to Forsyth Park – all different and filled with history, while claiming a place in the incredible design of the city. Do *not* miss the Cathedral of St. John the Baptist – one of the most breathtaking and brilliant places I have ever set foot inside. And, whatever you do, get to The Wilkes House for the meal of a lifetime.

Forsythe Park and the Savannah Squares… the St. John Cathedral… Mrs. Wilkes' Dining Room… the three must-do items of Savannah.

Some casual thoughts? Ok. Please stop in The Christmas Shop on Bull Street. Friendly people there. (Conveniently located near Madison Square… and very near St. John's.)

Go see at least one of the historic homes. I'd refer you to the Mercer House (actually called the Mercer-Williams House), but there are several worthy of note and I'm certain would offer a fascinating tour as Savannah's bygone days merge with current events.

I could go on… but that is the perfect start. You can build from there.

Because when it comes to Savannah… I can't tell you that you will have an incredible time on your visit. I wish I could. I can't. That's going to be up to you, and how you decide to experience it. What I can tell you is that this city is amazing and wonderful… you just might need to be open and flexible with your expectations and plans.

A never again moment

It's the middle of the afternoon on a gorgeous autumn day. You're walking through one of your favorite spots. Perhaps a path running within a quiet and wooded area. Perhaps it passes along the side of a river. You stop for a moment, take a deep breath, and look around.

Beautiful.

And there you are, standing silently, when a wave of realization sweeps over you...

This moment will never happen again.

The usual setting for my moments of realization involves waterfalls. For some reason, as a gorgeous cascade crests and tumbles, it strikes me that each and every second is absolutely unique. The water will never, ever, be in that formation again. It's there... it falls... it's gone. At no point to happen one more time.

A few years ago, Terry and I spent a weekend in New Hampshire. We decided to trudge along a snow-covered trail near a landmark called Diana's Baths. From parking lot to the falls is a beautiful walk of about a half-mile. And as we arrived, with the setting framed in a virtually untouched blanket of white, that realization moment struck. Not many people would ever see this sight. And even those that have visited the Baths (or will in the future) would never get to share this specific display.

Moments such as that don't need to be immediate however. Each sunset is unique… each evening spent with friends. And so many are worthy of our attention. How many holidays will we share with families? How many birthdays will we celebrate with friends? When added together, quite likely not nearly as many as we would like to think.

Often the most significant moments in our lives are easy to spot. We open our eyes and watch as the memories unfold before us. Many times we bring gifts for the festivities, take pictures of the travels, and ride the waves of emotions.

Harder to spot are those unexpected waterfall moments… ones were a set of circumstances came together to create something that will never again be repeated.

In December of every year, a bunch of us will be reminded that we've lost touch with a portion of our world. We'll head out to the store and buy a few boxes of cards, arrive at home and take out an address book, and begin writing on envelopes while realizing it's been too long since we've been in touch with many of the people we check off our list. A few of us will even promise to try and do better next year with our phone calls and e-mails and text messages. (And we actually mean it.)

Life though… it's funny.

We have a way of being naïve and acting almost numb to the realities around us. Try as we might, most of us will never share as many moments with our family and friends as we would like. And yet, each day we tend to rationalize what we can put off until tomorrow... until next week... until the weather gets better or our schedule opens up or whatever needs to happen to kick us into motion.

And that's ok. Life is meant to be lived, and we don't get to do everything we want where we want no matter how we wish we could. Which makes the trick learning to appreciate the moments you can enjoy, share and be a part of.

Every moment holds the potential of a waterfall experience. So pick up the phone, send a card, or head outside. Enjoy.

If you've taken a few moments over the years to explore my web site, you may have noticed that Harry Chapin is a personal favorite of mine ... both for his work as a musician and as an example of trying to make the world a better place. The organization World Hunger Year (WHY, founded by Harry Chapin) does incredible things, including annual Hungerthon efforts. You can learn more about the group at the WHY web site. Here, I would like to take a few minutes to reflect and consider ...

Would Harry Chapin be proud?

"This year's food drive was an overwhelming success, but we have just one problem and we're going to address it. Next week we're canceling all of our classes and we're going to talk about what these families are going to eat next week."
        ~ Harry Chapin on a "sensible" education
                                        system

It's been over twenty years since the world lost Harry Chapin, and it isn't that far-fetched to believe that if he were alive today, he wouldn't have let the arrival of a new millennium pass without making several comments on the state of the planet and the nature of man. So as Thanksgiving 2003 nears, would Chapin be proud of the way things are going?

On Tuesday, November 7, 2000, the United States of America held a national election to select a new president. In the 1996 presidential election, history was made when less than half of eligible Americans voted.

As a measure of apathy, it would appear that Chapin might have just cause for concern. After all, if a country can't get half of its people to vote for what is acknowledged as "the leader of the free world," than how can they be expected to make a difference in the lives of those less fortunate? As a group, it's very difficult to look at the picture of mankind and find it to be motivated beyond personal interests and self-serving efforts.

In the song "I wonder what would happen to this world", Chapin asks the listener to picture a world where every individual tried to accomplish everything they were capable of achieving. At concerts, he often told his audience that there was a difference between the upper, middle and lower classes. He said that the upper class couldn't be counted on for help because they didn't want to spend their money. The lower class had too many issues to be worried about personally to offer any assistance to others. Chapin concludes that it is up to the people in the middle class to make the difference. But, in the end, what Chapin in his casual comments truly seems to be recognizing is, that beyond wealth, race, age, or any other defining classification, it is the individual and the contributions made to the world by that person that make the difference. Is the world better because this person is here than it would be if this person weren't?

Ask any fan of Harry Chapin how they feel about him and his efforts and, though there may be several answers, one will clearly be heard more than all others combined. "I miss him." Harry's closet friends acknowledge repeatedly that he was generous with his time and commitments to a fault. And yet, people that loved Harry Chapin loved the fact that he was accessible, that he was genuine, and that he was true to his beliefs. Thousands of people attended his shows, knowing there would be preachy moments but also knowing that he cared. His legacy lives on in the continuing efforts of World Hunger Year, which he helped to found. And his legacy lives on in the efforts of individuals that, without the stage Chapin had to speak from, try to make the world a better place not just for themselves, but for all those around.

Take a few minutes and consider where you are right now. And, if you can, send a dollar to a local soup kitchen. Donate a blanket to a homeless shelter. Give a can to a food drive. Do something to make the world around just a little bit better than it was five minutes ago. It doesn't take much effort to try, even once a year, to make Harry Chapin proud.

A very special commemorative collector's double issue edition

Every so often, I think about collectibles.
I have a few. And I'm pretty certain that almost all of us do. For the most part, they represent something of personal interest. Childhood memories… a particular writer a person enjoys… a fascination with history (or a specific time in it)… religious… cultural… family… and more.
Several people see dollar signs. Which, quite honestly, is a bit foolish. Not because things can't skyrocket in value, but instead for a very simple theory: If you decide to collect something because it has been identified as valuable to collect and preserve, it's too late to collect anything that will be of value.
Consider – Beanie Babies.
Consider – *Star Wars* toys.
How many of you have several plastic storage containers of Beanie Babies? (Come on. We're friends here.

You can admit it. We have a few in our house. (I could almost rest my case here. But let's move on...))

The reality is that virtually none of the *Star Wars* toys to come out following the original trilogy of films have significant value. And while that isn't completely true, it is true enough to support the theory. Very, very few of the toys (if any) released to the general public for the upcoming *Rogue One* will become worthy of a college education fund for your children or a retirement beach house in Hawaii. Just not happening.

I'm wandering along these paths today because of a magazine that recently arrived at my house. My wife and I have subscribed to *Entertainment Weekly* for years. It's something we enjoy for virtually no other reason than we do actually enjoy reading it.

One funny thing about the magazine is the number special issue releases. They send out the occasional double-issue... jam packed with goodness and fun, and basically serving as an announcement that the staff is getting a week off and you won't get your copy next Friday. They publish multi-cover collector's issues. And as the aforementioned *Rogue One* nears release, this particular issue was hailed as: "A rebellious special issue." (One that also apparently had two covers... Felicity Jones on both, with either the Death Star or Darth Vader in the background. The Darth Vader version was... get ready... "sold exclusively at Barnes & Noble" locations.)

Looking around my office, there are several things I believe might qualify as special and possibly even collectible. Of course, each item is in some way special to me. They represent memories and travels and family and friends and just in general make me smile. The glass jug from Byrne Dairy? The stuffed Chip doll with the Rescue Rangers name pin? Great memories. Awesome memories. If I trade either for cash in about twenty years though, I'll still be just a tad short in my down payment on an Aston Martin. Doesn't make either less valuable or less meaningful to me.

But that collectors' market we hear so much about. The reality there is simple… if someone tells you something is special and collectible and they have an interest in getting you to look for it, chances are really good it probably isn't that special or collectible.

Amazing thing about supply and demand. There are actually multiple levels to it. It's never as simple as how much is available playing against how much is desired. For someone that has saved every issue of *Entertainment Weekly*, a trip to Barnes & Noble was in order. For me, not so much. Perhaps though—just *perhaps*—there is as much to be said about a smile as there is about an investment when it comes to collecting.

Merry Christmas... and I mean that

Merry Christmas everyone. All the best of the holiday season to you and your family... and my hopes for a happy and healthy New Year.

But mostly... Merry Christmas.

I have a lot of problems with the drive for correctness in the world. I am willing to admit, a good portion of my feelings stem from potentially misguided or far too personal thoughts and preferences. However, at the heart of all of my opinions is a very simple, very important little nugget of honesty... and we can use the Christmas spirit as a terrific example of that honesty.

My wishes are well-intended.

(Ok... I have some explaining to do. Before I start, please take your hands off the keyboard. Don't get too close to the e-mail option... don't be prepared to react immediately and strongly to what I'm about to say. Ok? Good. Here we go...)

The phrase "Merry Christmas" has, approximately, between zero and no religious meaning to me.

None at all.

The debate of history, and the primary focus of that history on religion... or why the date gained significance on, at least, the calendars of the American government, business world and educational system... is valid for exploring and understanding. However, whether the use of Christmas as the holiday... stress on *THE* holiday... is right, wrong, misguided, offensive, ignorant, insensitive or whatever else isn't in any way, shape or form valid in comprehending my wishes when I say "Merry Christmas" to you.

I want you to consider something a bit off-center of the day. For instance, like it or not, there is plenty of debate as to whether or not the origins of Christmas have anything to do with Jesus. The government uses it as a reference point. Businesses use it as a date for closing doors. Schools have it on their calendar. And many upon many reasons the date has significance have no true religious elements involved.

Call me sappy... sentimental... naïve...

I believe that each of us has the power to make a difference in the lives of others. And I believe that power is based on positive actions. Efforts that are selfless. Desires that are, both by intentional definition and the lack of better phrasing, pure.

And to those beliefs, I wish a Merry Christmas because I truly wish the best of these days. That you and your family are happy, healthy and safe. That these moments find you spending time and sharing experiences with those closest to you. That 2010 ends on a high note, 2011 is better than 2010, and 2012 may be better than 2011.

I wish a Merry Christmas because I truly believe we all can fulfill the promises of treating each other with kindness and compassion. That we can provide for those that cannot provide for themselves. That we can raise the standing of everyone by helping to lift the standing and comfort of others. That we can tear down meaningless boundaries and differences of separation to find strengths and accomplishments of unity.

I wish a Merry Christmas... Season's Greetings... Happy Holidays... or whatever words pass my lips because I care about you. Not because of any specific reason such as a common calendar of events or holidays or whatever... but because you are special and unique and matter.

Yes... call me sappy... call me sentimental... call me naïve... and I welcome it all.

When I wish you a Merry Christmas I am wishing you the greatest of gifts that any man could offer to another... recognition that you are important and deserve respect. And at one time of the year we can all put aside differences and disagreements, and find a way to embrace peace and tolerance.

I don't have to share a common element of any kind with you... I don't have to desire to spend time with you... I don't have to communicate with you... to honestly and sincerely hope that you are well.

Call me a fool for still believing in Santa Claus. Call me crazy for debating the merits of multi-colored lights versus single-color strands.

I understand.

On this holiday I wish you and your family a Merry Christmas.

I deliberately and proudly use those very words.

Not because December 25th does or does not have any special significance to you or to me. Not because you do or do not celebrate it. Not because you will or won't be working.

I use those words because, for me, they characterize great intentions of mine for you, your family, and your loved ones.

I wish you a Merry Christmas… and a Happy New Year.

…and always include a chocolate Santa

The Christmas season has begun.
(I know. For some stores it began about 16 weeks ago.)
It's a weird summary, and maybe when dealing with leaves and snow it's a northern summary to be sure, but it just seems that Turkey Day is a more realistic corner to turn and directly face the December festivities.
And with Thanksgiving behind us… when you are no longer considering the advertising and the everything else arriving far too early, and are instead focused on the holiday and holiday events… I think we can all agree that the rush to Santa Claus is now on.
Once you clear Thanksgiving, the get togethers… be it family or friends (or work)… tend to involve the holiday season. The weather begins to make a more significant turn from fall to winter. If not with snow, then with the ground getting harder and the days so much shorter.

Once you get past Thanksgiving, the leaves should be raked, and your outdoor Christmas decorations pretty much in place. A Christmas tree? Sure... and if you get a live one, even the earliest of decorators tend to purchase it over the long Thanksgiving weekend and not before.

And the pace picks up for shopping. Not all shopping mind you... but if you expect to find stocking stuffers and certain items, once November is gone the chocolate Santas tend to be disappearing as well. Buying a chocolate Santa on December 1st may seem early... but if you don't know the perfect chocolate specialty shop, just try finding a good one after the 15th.

Obviously this isn't perfect. But the general idea I'm trying to approach is based on a realistic atmosphere and not the artificial mass consumerism.

There are people that will tell you they know when it's going to snow... some say they can smell it in the air. And I do know what they mean. It's not enough for it to be overcast on a day when you can see your breath. That doesn't make snow. There's almost a static electricity feel in the air for some snow storms. There's something different about it... almost a taste, or perhaps even more, almost a sensory overload.

And so it is when the calendar is being flipped from November to December. You can sense the real thing appearing. Shopping and icicle lights don't make Christmas. There's something different about it.

This is the season when most family and friends tend to think about each other... remember those they may wish they had better communication or contact with... and hold gatherings. Weekends fill up. Days fly by.

And then arrive the traditions.

Some of my friends always have an orange in their stocking. A few claim to get at least one piece of coal... an arrangement with Santa that explains while you were good overall, there were some moments where you could have been better.

Some believe in wrapping all of the presents in a stocking… some open a present (or more) on Christmas Eve… some watch *A Christmas Story*. And somehow, Santa Claus and The Christmas Kangaroo remain true to the intentions beyond the different ways of celebrating.

For me and my family, it's always been a chocolate Santa. (Although, if you know my mother, the funny thing is… when it comes to several holidays, such as Thanksgiving, Christmas and Easter… you know that a lot of our family traditions and histories and memories are sealed with chocolate. From my family – I recall the great Easter Bunny trials… when someone was stealing bites from my chocolate bunny. I've witnessed phone calls, e-mails, and all sorts of covert operations invested in the planning of acquiring the ideal chocolate Santa.)

I know we all put a lot of time and attention into some incredible thoughts and expressions around Christmas. And some wander off into lands of political correctness and commercialism where many of us really shouldn't look.

How evil is it really to wish someone a Merry Christmas?

What date actually is appropriate for the first appearances of merchandise on store shelves?

You get the idea. For many, so much seems to happen every year that takes away from the true spirit of the season. And the marketing machine would have you believe that as Labor Day ends… well… it's ok for the same timing that indicates that white shoes must be put away to also signal breaking out the inflatable reindeer at low discount prices and for the holiday decorating of stores to begin.

Nonsense.

(And that's putting it kindly.)

The reality is simple... in two words... intent and tradition.

While I believe in Christmas lists and putting thought into gifts, I am not one for seeing Rudolph much before November is well underway.

If you are saying "Merry Christmas" because you are wishing the best for people, in sincere fashion, then I applaud you. I encourage such behavior. But for most that complain people are saying "Happy Holidays" because of some need to prove a perceived hidden agenda, then I have two completely different words to phrase my thoughts.

The intent is supposed to be about finding the best... the best of family... the best of friends... the best of neighbors... the best of mankind.

Traditions... parties and meals, presents and embraces... not only provide for cherished memories, but also complete the celebrations with moments and images.

There is a plastic Santa Claus face that occasionally makes an appearance on the house I grew up in. My Dad found it. Not sure where. (He seems quite proud of it. Not sure why.) If he was given it for free, he paid too much. And it became the punchline of many jokes. Many, many, *many* jokes. Until the year he decided not to bring it upstairs. Until the year he thought he wouldn't decorate with it. Because that year, everyone wanted to know where it was.

They may be funny. They may be annual moments acted out across generations. As this Christmas season begins, I once again wish the very best of them to you.

I hope you find happiness. I hope you find yourself exactly where you wish to be, and I hope you arrive exactly when you need to be there.

I wish you a Merry Christmas... and a chocolate Santa.

Resolutions and K-cups

The time is upon us where many people—read: most (and honestly, almost all)—will attempt to map out better things for the New Year.

I don't say "almost all" lightly. Because I think, at least to a small degree, all of us do find something appealing in the concepts of increased efforts, fresh approaches, and new beginnings. Even for those that may fall into the most cynical and pessimistic of attitudes can at least appreciate the idea of something different being both tempting and exciting.

Today though, my train of thought is running a bit off the tracks into a different direction. There is an action… the idea of change and improvement. I'm wondering about reaction… what happens because of and after the change.

As we all know, the humor of the resolution idea is found in the area that most people don't change. We sign up for gym memberships, then stop heading to our workouts before the second monthly payment is due. We declare our intentions for healthy eating, then add ice cream and cookies to our shopping carts by the second or third trip out for groceries that follows. We yearn for improved communication with family and friends, then before long arrive back at habits of rolling our eyes at text messages… delaying responses to e-mails… screening phone calls.

It's so easy to find the jokes wedged inside the realities. Deeper though, around a corner and hidden from view, is a stranger concept. Not just that we don't change… but instead a moment for considering if all change is good.

To show that concept, I need to make some coffee.

I've got a Keurig coffee maker. A lot of people do. I was introduced to it years ago, with my first unit being a very basic model, the old B31.

For me, the reasons I liked the Keurig were simple enough. It was founded on a combination of things: (1) I am the only person in the house that really drinks coffee. (2) I don't drink coffee daily, and often go several days between cups. (3) When I do have some, I usually only have one cup and rarely will I go beyond two. Easy enough to bring these (and a few other random ideas) together: when I drank coffee at home, I needed one cup and just about never anything approaching a full pot.

Then… my B31 broke down.

The replacement turned out to be a Keurig B130. And, for the most part, it's fine.

But that's it.

Fine.

Just, fine.

What I find fascinating though, is the differences between the B31 and the B130. And to this, I want to specifically bring your attention to removing and discarding the used pods.

With the B31, you simply flip the handle, pull out the used K-cup, discard that pod and close the unit. Not so with the B130.

There is a cycle involved. Opening to insert K-cup, closing compartment which automatically triggers the opening of the top panel so you can add water, the closing of the water area panel which triggers the request to start the brewing cycle.

And with the B130, even if all you want to do is clean up the unit and put it away, in order to remove a used K-cup you need to go through the entire process, including playing with the fill area for water and turning the unit off because it auto-started and wants to start brewing. You open the pod area, you start the full cycle.

Never mind the idea that the unit won't work unless a cup is in place. (This annoys me, since I like starting the process and then getting the cup ready with cream and sugar. But, I do get this one from a safety perspective, since it means the unit shouldn't spray hot liquids all over the place because you didn't get a cup in place at the dispenser.) Like other changes that occur between models and over time, I get that the B130 isn't going to operate exactly like the B31 or other Keurig units. No worries there. (Side issue – I can't prove as fact that the coffee is not as hot once brewed by the B130 as opposed to the B31. But I do find myself using the microwave to reheat a cup quite often, and usually pretty quickly after getting it. Problems that don't seem to happen when visiting my parents and using theirs, which remains a version of the B31. Anyway...)

Why the full operational cycle, every time? If you make just a single cup and want to store the unit cleanly, that means running through the process twice. It's a wear and tear waste on moving parts. It means needing to turn it off because you removed a pod... or at least double-checking to make sure the auto-timer turned things off when it ultimately wasn't used. And... well... look, I don't see the point.

Which... with a bit of ground left to cover... brings us back to resolutions.

I moved from the B31 to the B130 with good intentions. Something was broken, I wanted it in my life, and I moved to replace it. In a really stretched way, with several allowances to fit our tale, it was exactly what a person does with their resolutions.

I'm not here to tell you that getting some extra physical activity into your life, making good decisions about the food you eat, and improving your interactions with people are in any way bad things. Nope, not the point.

Instead, I just wonder if we're even slightly aware of what happens once we make these changes in our routines. Different does not always mean better. Operational does not always mean functional. New does not equal improved.

And I think those ideas... different, operational and new, placed against better, functional and improved... are really important when it comes to our resolutions and future endeavors. We crave better and improved, while usually fearing different and new.

It's a strange combination... a strange relationship... strange results.

Happy New Year.

Great in New York

I saw a quote on Facebook a few months ago. Went something like this (I'm paraphrasing): "Great quarterbacks don't lose two Super Bowls."

It was a shot against Brady.

Now I have several problems with that quote. But the reality is, simple and easy, it's a stupid thought. Without much research, my initial grasps on the issue quickly came to a few conclusions...

First – I can think of several average quarterbacks that have won a Super Bowl. I can think of more than several that have lost a Super Bowl. But I don't know many average quarterbacks that have led teams to more than one Super Bowl appearance.

Second – Granted, losing two titles does damage any person that wants to name Brady the greatest quarterback ever. Multiple titles and no championship defeats serves Joe Montana well in the debate. But getting to five Super Bowls and winning three will kind of make a career pretty special, even with two losses.

The more I thought about the idea, the more I was reminded a story…

A friend of mine was participating in a class-like discussion about baseball. As I recall, it was sort of a history class. And one day, the instructor posed a challenge to the class: "Define great."

My friend quickly responded: "Good in New York."

We'll come back to this. For now, let's get some information out there that will be valuable to our exploration. It's a chart of the past fifteen Super Bowls, featuring both teams and the starting quarterbacks.

Winning Team	Winning Quarterback	Losing Team	Losing Quarterback
New York (Giants)	Eli Manning	New England	Tom Brady
Green Bay	Aaron Rodgers	Pittsburgh	Ben Roethlisberger
New Orleans	Drew Brees	Indianapolis	Peyton Manning
Pittsburgh	Ben Roethlisberger	Arizona	Kurt Warner
New York (Giants)	Eli Manning	New England	Tom Brady

Indianapolis	Peyton Manning	Chicago	Rex Grossman
Pittsburgh	Ben Roethlisberger	Seattle	Matt Hasselbeck
New England	Tom Brady	Philadelphia	Donovan McNabb
New England	Tom Brady	Carolina	Jake Delhomme
Tampa Bay	Brad Johnson	Oakland	Rich Gannon
New England	Tom Brady	St. Louis	Kurt Warner
Baltimore	Trent Dilfer	New York (Giants)	Kerry Collins
St. Louis	Kurt Warner	Tennessee	Steve McNair
Denver	John Elway	Atlanta	Chris Chandler
Denver	John Elway	Green Bay	Brett Favre

Here are two things that stand out to me on that chart:

First – It's been nine title games since the last "not great" quarterback won. That would be Brad Johnson with Tampa Bay. Before that it would be Trent Dilfer with Baltimore.

I deliberately went back fifteen years instead of ten so we could get Kurt Warner onto our chart as a winner... because he's twice a loser, and we are talking about a "great quarterbacks not losing" theme as the basis of the column. (Plus he's also so wonderfully intertwined in the development of the Giants and their two championships when you think about it.) The funny thing that happened as a result was adding Trent Dilfer... and John Elway. Dilfer drops the 90% great margin down to 85%. But, once you see Elway's name there, you begin to realize even more strongly that the past decade... two decades... three decades aren't exactly rigged results in favor of great winners. The five winning quarterbacks before Elway include Brett Favre, Troy Aikman and Steve Young. Losing quarterbacks in the past twenty-five years bring in those four appearances from Buffalo and Jim Kelly. Plus... before winning his championships, I think we all recall the reputation Elway had.

Sure, the longer we go back the more likely we are to get a Mark Rypien as a winner... yet that also leads to the decade dominated by Joe Montana. In Super Bowls twenty-four and earlier we have Montana with four rings, Bradshaw with four, Starr with two and Staubach with two... which is four quarterbacks and twelve titles without getting to a full list of who started and was playing for the losing squads. (By the way... you might want to recall Staubach lost multiple title games as well.)

I feel comfortable saying that more often than not, especially when discussing quarterbacks that have more than one championship – if you had to bet you should place your money on great quarterbacks winning titles.

Doesn't completely answer our original quote though... does it? So...

Second – Check out the list of losing quarterbacks in the past fifteen games. I would say several of the losing quarterbacks qualify for any list of greats. In the past five years Peyton Manning, Ben Roethlisberger and Kurt Warner have each lost once, and Brady has lost twice. (And, as I sort of noted, Warner also has a second loss outside the recent five-year stretch.)

McNair isn't great, but he won an MVP award. Toss in Favre with Manning, Roethlisberger, Warner and Brady, and we arrive with a count that shows just shy of half the losers in the past fifteen years are: (1) also Super Bowl winners, and, (2) worthy of consideration as great.

Do we consider Jake Delhomme, Donovan McNabb, Chris Chandler and so on great? Nope... and they also all have in common just a single Super Bowl appearance. They never got a chance to play multiple times in the championship game.

And what we have arrived at is pretty interesting...

History shows us that many quarterbacks have made it to just a single Super Bowl. A few of those have victories, and the rest have losses. Most of the starting quarterbacks that have brought a team (or, Warner considered, we need to say teams) to more than one Super Bowl though: (1) have at least one victory, (2) are generally accepted as one of the greatest in history.

So... get a franchise to five Super Bowls with multiple titles... and yeah, I think we can say that a great quarterback has lost two (or more Super Bowls).

Look... you want to argue that Jim Kelly isn't great... I'm listening. Four Super Bowls and no titles. It's a Dan Marino type of argument that great doesn't have to come with rings. Got it.

You could argue that Kurt Warner isn't great... and once again, I'm listening. Three title games though, with two organizations and some MVP hardware says he was pretty darn good.

Roger Staubach though... he lost twice to Pittsburgh... and I would consider him one of the greatest. (Not top five of all-time greatest if you make the list today... but still one of the greatest.)

The end result is easy to see... lousy quarterbacks don't make multiple Super Bowl visits. And when you begin talking about three... four... five opportunities... we are in some rarified air.

Yup, Brady's legacy does in fact include a missed opportunity at perfection. He has lost his two latest chances at a fourth title. But losing two does not mean he isn't great. In fact... there's a good chance it means exactly the opposite. It's pretty special that he quarterbacked a team to two losses.

I'm my own barista

Just watching TV the other day, and oh… dear… lord… NO!

"I'm my own barista."

It was an advertisement for a local gas, convenience, all-in-one-quick-mart store. And, the specific focus of the ad was the beverage center inside. More specifically: the coffee.

My reaction really isn't quite as extreme as an exclamation point following a capitalized "NO" might suggest… because the reaction wasn't for the barista comment on its own. It was directed more toward what the designers and creators let get past them in commercials these days on the whole rather than one specific moment. (Or, at least what they create.)

I've reacted to several of these in the past few months. The trigger moment here was the self-proclaimed barista though. Ok... perhaps a bit more on it...

They were basically running five second blurbs from the just-like-you-and-me folks. Started off with a quick shot of the store with an intro, and then a cut to the customers. This man likes his French vanilla, and that woman likes the convenience she finds, and so on. And then... then we are treated to this guy...

"I'm my own barista."

And—wish I was kidding—he was *SO EXCITED* about being his own barista that it was frightening. I stopped wondering about cups of coffee and was scared.

And if you think I might be exaggerating, since... sure... I screamed "NO!" a few moments ago, you would be wrong. I, literally, would be terrified to meet this guy in person if he behaved the way he looked while telling me how great it was that he could be his own barista. So terrified that as I consider it, I think it just might actually be stunning and worthy of capital letters, since his excitement... hold on... new paragraph...

You get that he was beyond deliriously happy about going to the convenience store because apparently they let him make his own coffee, right? That's what being your own barista is. No... no... please understand as you debate me that making his own coffee is pretty much exactly the most basic interpretation. Professional baristas are more than that... and many have some incredible talents. But given the presentation of this guy in this setting, I think it's pretty safe to say it: Being your own barista is equal to making your own cup of coffee.

I said that on its own, the ad likely wasn't worth the startling "NO!" I offered. And that's probably a fair critique if you wanted to argue the point. After all... if I was able to show the video to everyone and tally some sort of "what did you see here" comments... if I contacted the writer and director and everyday-customer-excitement-barista-guy... the guy might just be excited because all the flavors and options and equipment and more... we might find that he doesn't have all this coffee-making-stuff in his own home, he comes to this store for everything it offers, and he feels just like a professional barista. Perhaps I would find that I'm on the outside on this one.

(On the other hand, we might also learn that a majority of people agree with me. Perhaps others see a look in his eyes similar to what we would expect to find in the eyes of a serial killer that has just spotted a car up ahead and off to the side on a dark, deserted road. (It was a very strange look of excitement. Really. It was.))

But I want to approach that production team... the creators of the ad... for different reasons. Do they offer it up to someone for review? Is there a person, without an opinion or an interest in the results, that takes a look at it? Do they do any research to find out what might go wrong?

And the likely answers are... no... no... and NO.

Several weeks ago, a different commercial set me off when a woman was speaking about her new car. She was so happy because... hold on, I'm not sure you're ready for this. Sit down. Ok. Think you're all set? Here we go:

> "...I get up hills that I never could get up before, park in parking spots that I would have gotten stuck in..."

Yes, indeed, she was over the moon because she could park her car.

Quite often, I've found that there are two things that serve me well in addressing any problem I have, headache I'm experiencing, or answer I'm trying to find.

First – Follow the money. This one is simple. The biggest motivation for doing anything is money. Want to know why someone is doing anything? Check the dollars first.

Second – Look in the mirror. You really need to be willing to ask about yourself in any scenario. It's quite possible that you are all alone in your thoughts. Others might not feel the same way you do.

Both of these might be worthy of an essay, or even essays, exploring the ups and downs and possibilities. This is not that essay.

Instead, I'm just wondering about marketing teams and what we are led to believe are professionals when the messages being delivered are that a person is excited about the self-service opportunities or that their vehicle can get out of a parking space. The money... the mirror... check and check... I'm not alone in finding myself completely unmoved about heading out for coffee or to make a new car purchase, so it isn't me and there has to be something else at play.

Of course, the third item on the list probably should be that remembering that common sense is not that common. Shaking my head in disbelief is an acceptable reaction. And perhaps, that some thought based on common sense should be first on the list. Unfortunately, none of that would answer why this guy can't make a cup of coffee at home.

Is the war on terror bringing us to *1984*?

I was reading an article from the *Herald Sun* in Australia. In Melbourne, it is estimated that just about every person appears on surveillance cameras one hundred or more times *per day*.

Now I want to be both realistic and, in a way, conservative in approaching such a number.

First of all, I think that we can agree just about the only place that does not have surveillance cameras of some kind is our respective homes. Perhaps you have them at your house, but for most people I'm going to say no, and I firmly believe we can all say that's accurate. But the grocery store... the bank... even at the places we work... it's possible. Once we get into our cars and leave the driveway, or close the door on our apartment, there is a chance that we are being watched on a surveillance camera. I think that's being realistic.

Secondly, I think it's safe to say that most people are in their homes for about twelve hours a day. I know that doesn't apply in every case… some are home more often… some are home less often… and for some it all depends on the day of the week. But between sleeping, eating and just watching television or whatever we do to occupy our time, twelve hours in the house seems like a safe, conservative average.

Ok so far? Good…

That means… by doing the math… that most of us are in some way possibly being watched for half of every day. And if we can use this breakdown of a day as somewhat universal… which I think is fair… and are to believe the numbers being reported in Melbourne, that means they appear on a surveillance camera eight to ten times every hour. And that's the part of this report that I wonder about.

The article doesn't say what an "appearance" is.

Is it any place I go? Perhaps I show up on the tapes from two or three different cameras in the bank, but since it was just at the bank that only counts as a single appearance.

Is it any time I show up, even in the same place but on a different camera? I could be at a gas station or in a department store, and if I move into the range of three different cameras while there, even in a matter of seconds, that counts as three appearances.

Is it a length of time that I appear on camera? It could be the same camera that is watching me, but if it picks me up for over ten seconds… over thirty seconds… over a minute… that triggers a count as an additional appearance.

The differences between what an "appearance" is are important. Because by pushing examples like the ones I've noted to the extreme, eight to ten appearances per hour could range from filling the gas tank of my car and getting a drink at a convenience store (which might fill the quota for an entire hour in just a few minutes) to having a camera fixed inside the monitor of my computer on my desk at work.

But let's push this matter forward a bit, beyond who is watching, when they're watching, what they're watching and how long they're watching.

As the article mentioned, surveillance images have allowed for incredible advances... and amazingly quick advances... in assembling information about bombings in England. The article also mentions a degree of privacy concerns. And I think... well, I *think* everyone is overreacting a bit. And that scares me... because it sure seems like George Orwell may have only been off by a couple of decades.

The old cliché says there are two sides to every story. And in my experience, that's true. For every story... issue... debate... situation... circumstance... whatever... there are two sides. In most cases, they aren't in complete agreement. And of those cases, just about all of the time the truth is in the middle. (That however, would create a third story, and is a thought best saved for an entirely different essay.)

We want to live in a black and white, right and wrong world... where decisions are easy and the truth is obvious.

We don't.

We live in a world with varying shades of gray, and the truth being found in the middle of the two sides. Sure, it may reside closer to one story than it does to the other... but it's in the middle... in the gray.

As a result, quite often the immediate reactions to a problem aren't the best solutions. They tend to favor one side of the story or the other, and neglect to take into account that the real solution is also going to be found in the middle.

It's true that these surveillance cameras can be responsible for some great things. But for people that defend them in absolute terms, I ask you if you've heard of identity theft.

Yes.

Identity theft.

Because, as one example, twenty years ago when I was applying to colleges, every application had a place for my Social Security number. Didn't give it a second thought at the time. And now? Have you heard what happened at the University of Connecticut? I don't have the link, but it was directly from a UConn site and provided details about how approximately 72,000 people may have had information compromised. (I didn't go searching for a link that connected, because the story from UConn and information being compromised is simply far too common.)

Take that idea of providing information in what we approach without a second thought and run with it.

What about the financial institutions? Banks, credit reporting agencies, or any other place that holds such records. Do you pay attention to the news? Because it's filled with stories of records being stolen or in some way violated.

Do you think they thought about these possibilities when creating the idea of a Social Security number? How about all the organizations that decided to ask for an individual's Social Security number?

And the people that decided to computerize all of my data so that someone might be able to get it from a source I trusted? I'm just asking...

Because as we talk about these surveillance cameras, and see how they are being used for more and more and more things... from security in buildings to catching motor vehicle violations to any other purpose... it seems to me that the world today has more or less not only accepted them in certain instances, but accepted their importance in future uses.

The people claiming that we need more and more cameras are right... to a point. But having seen what protection my identity is offered, forgive me for not having complete and blind faith that the cameras will always be used for the right reasons.

The people claiming that our privacy is being violated and the need for more controls are right… to a point. But to paraphrase Sean Connery in *The Untouchables*… you don't bring a knife to a gunfight. If the technology is there to help deter crime, then it is a responsibility of society to in some way investigate that technology.

A few years ago, I was working in a place that cashed checks for people. In order to sign up for this, a patron would have to supply some information… such as identification and a Social Security number. A man came in looking to cash a check, but refused to provide his Social Security number. I apologized and told him we couldn't cash the check without it. And that's when the Abbott and Costello routine broke out.

He insisted I had to cash the check.

I insisted… as politely as I could… that I could only attempt to cash it with the required information.

He actually debated it with me for ten minutes. (Another example of another essay idea, for another time.)

He was absolutely right… he didn't need to give me the number. But he was wrong… I didn't have to cash his check.

If advances in the world… such as technology and surveillance cameras… are going to be made thoughtfully and responsibly, I can accept that. A few extra minutes is a small price to pay so I can go to the top of the Empire State Building or fly to Australia and feel safe. Figurative connection – if I want my check cashed, there may be some procedures I need to accept.

But if they are being planned only as a reaction to something, and if people think that the systems will never be abused or misused… well… that's wrong. And if that *is* the case, then we really are heading for a day when people will be watched for every second, every action and wondering where it all went wrong.

Middle of the road as time goes by

Time is a funny thing, isn't it?

A day consists of twenty-four hours… one thousand four hundred forty minutes… eighty-six thousand four hundred seconds… standard measures of time. One day.

Yet depending on a variety of things, a day can pass as if nothing more than a blink of an eye or drag along as if chained to cinder blocks.

A day… a week… a month… a year… moves along differently for those that are being punished or waiting for Santa Claus than it does for those that are beginning a vacation or working a nine-to-five job. Perspective, if nothing else, matters.

Occasionally we get to view some things through an interesting lens… the it's been longer since such and such concept. I'll give you an example of what I mean.

In July of 1985 a concert was held. Known as Live Aid, it involved performances pretty much around the world.

(Primarily in London and Philadelphia, though other events took place in several other cities and countries.)

One of the strange things that popped up as the event was covered was a comparison to Woodstock. The foundation of the comparison was basically the idea of a collection of mega-musical-talent sharing the same stage. (A better comparison might have been to the US Festivals… and since then, to any of a number of ellas and paloozas and more. But Live Aid to Woodstock, fine.)

Woodstock took place in August of 1969. That's roughly sixteen years before Live Aid.

This summer, we will be separated from Live Aid by thirty-two years. It has been twice as long between today and Live Aid as it was between Live Aid and Woodstock. I feel pretty good saying that none of the ellas and paloozas since quite match up to the historical standard-bearers.

I occasionally get struck by this thought in other ways. I am now long since beyond eighteen-years removed from my college graduation… meaning more time has passed since college ended than the length of time I lived before heading off to begin it.

Every so often we have these markers in our lives. Many of them are placed by others. They reflect accomplishments and recognition that we might say the general public has deemed significant. Earning a driver's license, voting and the ability to purchase alcohol are three good concepts for this.

Some of them are more personally assigned their status. Weddings and children and such fall into this area, along with special moments and accomplishments.

As life moves along, we find these moments disguised by time. Some are cherished. Some are forgotten. Some are stored away until discovered later. Their importance may never be questioned, but the time surrounding them becomes fascinating. As it approaches... as it's experienced... as it appears in the past.

My wife and I have been a couple for more than two decades, and this fall we'll hit the twentieth anniversary of our wedding... which means that depending on how you want to count, we have been together for about forty-percent of the years that my parents have been married. (Which hardly seems possible in so many ways... but yes, Mom and Dad and Fifty Years!)

I suppose part of my disbelief about these things is easy enough to understand... not many people want to place themselves squarely in middle age (or years beyond the moments). But perhaps there is even more to it...

A very good friend of the family said something interesting to me when I graduated from high school. He took me aside and offered words quite close to: "Bobby, some of the kids you walked across the stage with have already finished the best days of their lives."

Now *that's* scary... that so many people could close the book on their greatest moments before turning eighteen... scary, and quite true.

Regardless of our desire to use them for work, rest, entertainment or any other number of ideas, we all get the same measurements of time in general. Sixty seconds in a minute... sixty minutes in an hour... and so on. What we don't share equally is how many of those seconds we get to use. And perhaps that creates the strangest and most amazing wonder of all.

As today moves along, there will undoubtedly be a few things that I'll shift to a different to-do list. Something for tomorrow... something for later... something that may not get done at all. And I expect than many of those things I will ultimately get around to finishing at some point.

But as we reach certain milestones... as we place certain markers in our life... do we really recognize the accomplishments with an understanding of what we might actually be able to do? To paraphrase something Harry Chapin said... what if for one moment everyone tried to be the best they could be?

Ok... this isn't about making sure you pick up the phone the next time your mother calls... nor is it designed to create an appreciation for every cup of coffee you share with your father. It's not intended to motivate you to work and focus and more. I'm just wandering along the road and thinking about some of the billboards I've seen along the way. (And wondering a bit about the destinations yet to come.) Hopefully, I'll be smart enough to appreciate the journey.

The mom bag

1997. My wife, two stepsons and I are preparing for our first trip together. It was to be the first major vacation of any kind for the three of them. She has decided that everything must be accounted for, and two weeks prior to our departure, clothes and other items are starting to assemble in small but ever-growing piles. Shorts, socks, shirts and new toothbrushes. Two weeks' worth of clothes being stacked up and organized.

I thought she was nuts. Having mastered the shower-pack-and-out-the-door-for-the-weekend-in-under-thirty-minutes maneuver, I wasn't planning on having anything out until the day before we left. But, supportive and helpful I was in those days. So, when asked for the carry-on bags and luggage, a red backpack was placed with the supplies.

> *"What… is… that?"*
> *"My carry-on."*
> *"It isn't really going with us, is it?"*

"Yes."
"No, really, it isn't, right?"

Finally, concerned with other things, the red backpack got past her and was allowed to make the trip. Off to Florida.

During our first few days moving from theme park to theme park, the backpack offered bottled water, cameras, sunglasses, gum, maps, and held purchases. When I pulled out three sweatshirts one evening as the temperatures dropped, my wife looked stunned.

> *"You've had those with us all day?"*
> *"Yup."*
> *"We'll buy you a new bag when we get home. That one's dirty."*

1979. I first learned about the mom bag in September. My parents made a family outing an annual summer tradition. It usually involved camping with friends, or a trip in the northeast section of the United States such as around New England, Pennsylvania or New York. Never very far from our home in Rhode Island, although to the kids in the back of the station wagon, it was always far enough.

This trip was big time though. Disney World. A full week. During the school year. And as the family strolled around the Magic Kingdom, mom was the center of attention.

> *"Mom, do you have my hat?"*
> *"Mom, can you hold this for me?"*
> *"Mom, dad says you have the film."*

And on and on and on.

Where did mom keep all this wonderful stuff? In one of those big, canvas, shoulder bags... a square measuring a foot or so, and capable of comfortably holding more than a large suitcase. It became known as "the mom bag," and it joined us from that trip on.

1986. Syracuse, New York. I start carrying my life around in a blue backpack. It was used for my books. It was used it for weekend trips. The backpack was a book bag, overnight bag, camera bag, laundry bag, and shopping bag. Heck, since I put my walkman in it when I strolled between campus and my apartment, my backpack was even a stereo. During four years of college, the only change was replacing it with a red one of the exact same style for my senior year.

Over the years I've also had a slightly different "mom bag" of sorts as well. It's a drawer at my desk and a file on the computer. It's the place I've put dated material, unfinished pieces, and works in progress. The place where things get stored because there's no time to work on them or they just don't seem to be developing right. The place where stuff goes when one or more markets have passed on them, or when rejection letters have been returned concerning them, or I just can't revise them one more time.

From that physical bag in 1979 to the figurative bag of 2003, so goes the progression to *In My Backpack – the web site*. The material may not all be gems. Some of it may interest visitors to the site. Some of it won't. But it's stuff that I've pulled from those drawers and files. Stuff stored away in my backpack looking for a place and just waiting for its time. And when the night gets chilly, or the kids get thirsty, or someone has to carry that stuffed animal you had to buy, the backpack is ready.

The mom bag lives on. The wife has tried to remove its place as a carry-on over the years, but it always gets packed. And the material I've written has a home. Now I'm the keeper of the bag, lugging it and its contents around. It's not that heavy actually. And I hope you'll find that there's a sweatshirt or two here that fits.

Lintables, non-lintables and whites

There are way too many options out there for me today… and I'm pretty sure I'm not alone. As society advances and moves… ahem… forward, it seems like more and more things don't work as well as they did yesterday. Some would argue I'm just resistant to change. I say change isn't always for the best.

Take technology for instance.

Remote controls as a specific.

Just about all of us have at least one universal remote in the house. I think I have about seventy-five. One came with the television… another with the DirecTV… another with the DVD player… and yet another with the VCR. I also found one downstairs from the cable box. All of those were designed not only for the unit they were packaged and sold to me with, but also have the listing of codes that can be programmed in to operate other things.

The problem is… they never work. Well, almost never. And even if they do, they don't do everything they should.

Sure... I'll give you an example. In fact, I'll give you two... DirecTV and my VCR.

Just over two years ago, we brought DirecTV to our house. We love it… although I do need to note that Tigg's enthusiasm for the Sunday Ticket package of NFL games isn't quite as strong as mine. In August of 2003 we went on vacation. One of the two dogs… I'm guessing Travis… decided to eat our DirecTV remote.

We have a universal remote for our television set (I should say had a universal remote... Travis ate that one too and we had to order a replacement). But DirecTV had switched to a new brand for producing its receivers, and that brand wasn't compatible with the television remote's codes. I don't know about you… but those so-called learn features where you can teach a remote to do certain things are way too complex to try and figure out, and… usually don't work anyway (which is a part of my point).

What do I mean by not doing everything? Well…

I use the universal remote to run my VCR. The play button works. So do the fast forward, rewind and record buttons. But, the menu options don't work. Any time the power goes out, I need to original remote to set the clock. Any time I want to set the timer, I need the original remote to set the program details.

The universal remote never is an exact duplicate of the original… it's always missing a special button, or it only works for the main features.

So, my DirecTV remote that Travis ate? I did find one that worked for most of the options, but it isn't perfect.

My VCR options? I need to keep the original around.

And the technology that supposedly allows me to do so much... such as having just one remote for everything instead of five... is flawed.

But I didn't start this article to talk to you about remote controls. I started it because of my dirty laundry. Seriously... and literally... my dirty laundry.

I like to keep things simple. The talk about the remotes? Well, it was intended to point out that sometimes the more you try to improve things, the more you simply create other problems, which often are more complicated than just dealing with the inconvenience.

When I left for college, I had never done laundry that often. In trying to take in my mother's advice, while not ruining everything I had in the process, I developed my own way of washing my clothes. Three categories.

Lintables...

Non-lintables....

And whites.

The idea was actually pretty simple. Anything that would pick up fuzz if it was tossed in the dryer with towels was a lintable. Anything that could be put in the dryer with towels and wouldn't pick up fuzz was a non-lintable. And, anything that could be washed with bleach was a white.

Easy... right?

Well, I thought so to. But, just like the progression found in the history of universal remotes, the process for doing laundry has advanced over the years.

Clorox 2 was the first item as I recall... safe for colors. That one was ok I suppose. But from there we went from plain detergents to detergents with bleach, detergents with bleach alternatives, additive free detergents, and extra strength detergents. (Would you believe that Tide calls it's products the "fabric care network"? They do. (I got a good laugh out of that one, too.))

But it's Cheer that has me upset right now. Not because I don't like Cheer... it's absolutely fine. No... it's Cheer Dark Formula to be specific.

Would anyone be against them making their regular Cheer better at preventing the fading of colors? Probably not. I guess this is a special Cheer though... and regular Cheer shouldn't be confused with Cheer Dark. Right?

Wrong. They actually say on their web site that Cheer Dark is "great for your everyday wash."

It is? Then why isn't it just new and improved Cheer? Why do I have to stand in the laundry detergent aisle, look at all of the different brands of Tide, Cheer and so on, deciding between them all? Why do they want me buying several different kinds?

Please don't get me wrong... I understand some of the differences. Allergies for instance. I understand that many companies take certain allergies into account when making different kinds of detergents. That's fine.

But as with the promise of a universal remote, I can't help but feel that I'm the stupid one here. "You idiot... you've actually been doing laundry all along and were quite happy with the results provided from one bottle and a box of dryer sheets? You need to have powdered detergent to treat the mud stains and liquid detergent to pretreat stains. Everyone else knows this. Get some bleach for your whites, but have some alternatives for bleaching your colors too. Liquid fabric softener for the stuff that doesn't go in the dryer, and sheets for the stuff that does."

Where does the list end?

Actually... it doesn't...

It never ends. It's just another of the bigger and better mentality. The same mentality that brings us "new and improved" (and the subsequent joke... if it's new, how can it be improved... and if it's improved how can it be new…). But that's missing the point. In reality what they are saying to us is that it's better.

It's a universal remote. Try it. You'll be happier.

It's another thing to think of while doing your laundry. But keep buying the original stuff too, even though this will work fine on everything else.

Years ago, there was an episode of *M*A*S*H* where a visitor came to the 4077th. I believe it was Alan Alda's father, Robert, playing the part. (The research I did shows Robert Alda playing the role of Dr. Anthony Borelli in an episode called "The Consultant.") The visitor kept trying to get Hawkeye to do things differently… from his clothes to his drink. He did it with most of the people at the camp and kept saying things such as "…better, right?" when they tried it. And as I recall, they all got very tired of it. Some of it was better. Some of it was new. But it didn't change the fact that for most things… from keeping warm to getting drunk… they liked things pretty much the way they were.

Changes.

Sure. I shouldn't be so resistant to them. But please don't tell me that the new things are better when they don't do most of what the old things did. Please don't tell me things are improved when they still want to sell me the old stuff too. And please don't tell me things have to be different when I'm pretty happy with the way things are.

Picture-in-picture is great, but I could care less about it when all I want to do is set my VCR to record *Friends*. Picture-in-picture buttons are no help with that… and I set the timer far more often.

Cheer Dark… even though the stuff with colorguard was very good and you should still buy it.

Great.

If you'll excuse me… I have three loads of laundry to sort.

Slater Park

I remember a place that in the middle of a city was all alone. Once, Slater Park was in Pawtucket, but Pawtucket was not in Slater Park. As I drove in for a visit one day, the setting of trees became more dominating as the traffic along the main road moved further behind. To the right, a pond was shimmering in the glow of the sun. The zoo had an entrance up and off to the left, just beyond the World War II gun that pointed back toward the ducks and geese which surrounded the gazebo at the pond's distant end.

I pulled my car off to a small paved lot on the right, about one-hundred yards beyond the ducks. My grandfather used to bring me to this park years ago. We would come equipped with a bag filled with the ends from loaves of bread. The birds have noticed my approach, and seem confused. They waddled straight toward me, then, perhaps noticing nothing in my hands, appeared completely disinterested as they turned and passed.

When I was in high school I ran a cross country meet here. The race began at a set of tennis courts that hadn't existed during my days as a wide-eyed six-year old. My grandfather came to watch me run that day. It was the first time in several years we had been here together, and it would also be the last.

I got back in my car and drove ahead into the area near the zoo's doors. The city has undergone many changes recently, primarily through corruption and politics. The mayor was forced to resign when charged with extortion. He later pleaded guilty to the charges, which were based on his business dealings as a representative of the city. Recently, a friend told me of the plans to close the zoo portion of the park by the year's end. I needed to make at least one more visit. I had wondered how the construction of the past few years, coupled with the news of the closing, had affected all that existed inside the walls before me.

The place was barren. No children ran beyond the sound of their parent's call to return and stay close. No people wandered beside me through an afternoon of daydreams and fantasies. Just a few apathetic looking workers finishing up one assignment and preparing for news of their new location a month or two in the future. For them, like the animals, it seemed to be a change though the overall story remained the same.

I roamed outside for a little while, passing the deer exhibit. It used to be surrounded by a fence that was the only thing separating me from their battle for position as I forced more pieces of bread through to them. Now, a cement wall with bubble windows allowed me to watch the deer as they walked around the enclosure. I almost missed how wet my hand would get when I fed them.

I decided to sneak in and visit with Fanny, resident elephant, for a few minutes. The two of us were alone in the building. She didn't seem to recognize me. Her eyes looked in my direction, and as I stared into them, they appeared hollow and vacant. Her pen was too small, and here I understood how the zoo could be held in such low standing nationally. Not filled with sunny days of bread crusts with my grandfather, it was instead rated as one of the worst zoos in the country. I wished for the apple I used to feed Fanny, but perhaps it's best I didn't have one. Uniting that brilliant past with this day wasn't something I really wanted.

The entire state has changed in the past year. Credit unions were forced to close when the state insurance company for depositors went out of business after a series of poor investments and embezzlements. Many of the closed locations have yet to reopen, and may never do so. Rhode Island was targeted as a major money laundering area by the F.B.I. Even the elected mayor of Providence has a criminal record for assault, earned when he was last in the same office. The days of innocence in the eyes of a child were not to be found again.

My grandfather passed away recently, and maybe I was trying to recapture a small token of something I had lost. On this visit, I couldn't help but see that all the bad this state had been through in the past few years had somehow made its way even here. But in the memories I hold of visiting this place, I found that I have something that not even the park could claim.

Mom's kitchen

Made from scratch.

For those of us craving the foods coming out of the kitchens of our youth, those three words provide a sure sign of quality.

Mom's a scratch baker.

That's not quite fair... or accurate. She's actually a scratch cook. Virtually everything I can recall being made in our home while growing up was assembled in house.

For those that may not be familiar with the term, cooking from scratch basically is a simple way of saying that all of the ingredients were brought together at the same time. No add two eggs and a cup of water to the box mix cooking. And in my family home, while growing up rarely were elements taken out of packages or jars.

These days, I usually hear it referred to as homemade, with the term scratch being used less and less. But the weird thing is... homemade doesn't quite work as well. Watch enough cooking shows, and eventually the host will break something out of their pantry that was not made in their kitchen. Usually it's something like a pie crust, where you can almost excuse the use and allow for the homemade label. But I've seen cookie dough and cake mixes... bagged hash browns and taco seasoning packets... all brought forward and presented with a disclaimer saying there's nothing wrong with letting someone else do the hard work, clean up the mess, and save you time while you deliver a homemade meal.

And there's not anything wrong with that.

But that meal was not made from scratch. The homemade part isn't quite right.

Several years ago, I went out shopping with my twin nieces and nephew. They were visiting from Australia, were close in ages to 7 and 5, and we were getting the ingredients for an awesome sundae bar that was going to be the featured treat of the evening.

My mother would excuse the can of whipped cream I brought home. While she would have preferred a carton of heavy cream and doing the work in her own stand mixer, that item was understandable. But I had gone too far...

Jimmies and hot fudge and nuts and caramel sauce and cherries and... all delicious and wonderful options and... oh dear lord, NO... a roll of cookie dough? What the HECK was *THAT* doing in her house?

Yeah... well... it seemed as though the four of us had gotten a bit carried away in selecting flavors of ice cream and options ranging from banana splits to serving the sundae with warm cookies. As things were flying into the cart, I figured making a dozen or two cookies quickly from the roll would be a heck of lot quicker, with fewer counters and pans in use, than making a batch of cookies from scratch.

And my mother was shocked.

This was a woman that would make anything for her grandchildren. A woman I can readily picture over the years many times melting the unsweetened chocolate to make a batch of brownies. And I had invaded her territory with a roll of cookie dough.

Shame… shame… shame.

My how times have changed.

In my younger days, I spent time with my grandparents. And a funny thing about Meme and Pepe… some of the moments I recall them getting along the best were in the kitchen while making meat pies. Actually… pork pies… and more specifically, *French* pork pies.

Now, truth be told, having been in the kitchen often with Terry… to results of both amazing meals created with wonderful choreography as well as good food somehow created while tripping all over each other… I can look back at my grandparents with a bit more clarity and understanding provided by age and experience. Chances are pretty good one of the secrets involved in the French pork pie kitchen harmony was one working on the filling while the other made the crust. Still…

From scratch.

How I wish I could sit in the corner of the kitchen watching them work on the pies one more time. Which in turn brings us back to Mom.

So often we talk about the special ingredient… love.

Is it harder to make things from scratch in the kitchen? Many times… no. You might need to be aware of things when you go shopping. But in most general recipes, we are probably talking about saving seconds and not hours. We probably are not creating any extra dirty dishes. Just a matter of grabbing a few spice bottles instead of tearing open a seasoning pack.

Looking back though… Thanksgivings and holiday parties… birthday cakes and summer cookouts… the food was outstanding. And part of that magic was the prep work... the scratch work... the watching and helping to make everything from beginning to end work.

That concept hasn't truly been lost. Making jellies and salsas and finding unique ways to take advantage of everything coming out of the garden (while plotting to plant something new next year), creates a similar thoughtfulness and batch of memories. People do still make things at home.

But the scratch term doesn't seem to be there. The family connections between generations aren't exactly the same. There's an ingredient missing and I'm not sure what it is. I won't be sappy and say it's the love. But when you consider what makes a house a home, there needs to be a slightly different but very similar allowance... and appreciation... for the deeper meanings of homemade.

Stone wall chipmunks

I understand the thing about the goldfish now.

Out in my front yard there is a stone wall. It becomes one of those fairly well-formed retaining walls when it turns and follows the driveway to the house. But along the front, on both sides of the driveway, it has that old look. Round stones and flat stones, with gaps and spaces and a couple of places that appear ready to fall.

And it has chipmunks.

I don't know how many are living there, but there is at least one on each side. I know this only because one time I saw two chipmunks, facing each other from opposite walls at the edge of the driveway.

A few weeks ago, I sat and watched.

I was having a particularly miserable day. Couldn't focus on my writing. Had a honey-do list where every item was fighting me and taking twice as long to finish as it should. And it was almost time to head into the kitchen to make dinner. Having spent the better part of two hours fighting with a lawn mower that didn't want to run, I sat down on the front steps.

A head popped into view.

Over about five minutes, we both adjusted our positions. I moved down the driveway and sat on the wall about twenty feet from the chipmunk. It moved to the top of the wall and then stood pretty much still, only occasionally turning its head. And for perhaps ten minutes, I just stared.

I'm not going to tell you I had some sort of tremendous moment here.

I was watching a chipmunk.

But all those stories of how watching fish in an aquarium can lower blood pressure suddenly make sense. Because I felt better after spending some time with this chipmunk. I felt better for no reason at all.

And when my new friend dove back into the wall, I turned and went back to the house, to push my headache of a lawnmower into the garage.

Back to the house with a new appreciation for smelling the roses and enjoying the quiet, little moments as they pass.

I take great pride in both of my four-legged children… Lady and Travis… the Labradors. Those of you that know her will be happy to hear that a very healthy Lady has passed her eleventh birthday. Travis is closing in on his sixth. When I come home from work, there they are… tails wagging, looking up at me, fighting for prime position for the welcome home head scratches. Every dog lover out there understands the "we are *so glad* to see you" tap dance that goes on. Makes for a great transition between the work day and the evening.

Makes a house a home.

I really don't have much of a point for this essay. I wasn't sure if I would find one as I wrote it. I'm not sure that I've found one now that I'm almost done. But when I arrived at home this evening and came around the corner into the driveway, a chipmunk sprinted under some leaves and over a rock.

And I smiled.

Then I got to the back door, opened it up, and was almost knocked to the ground by jumping dogs.

And I smiled again.

Right now, as I finish this, Travis is curled up around my feet, and Lady is in the bedroom warming up Tigg's side.

Life is good.

And I have the chipmunks to thank for pointing that out.

A shock to the system

Last week, Terry and I were doing some work in the yard.

For the major items on our list, we planted some holly and moved some lilacs. After that, we began an assortment of smaller projects that involved just about anything in light landscaping from pruning this tree to removing that plant and more. And as we considered what to add, adjust, or take away, a thought occurred to me...

Plants are a lot like people.

When we first began moving into our new house, we made an effort to bring along a few special items... a few of the irises given to us years ago by a delightful neighbor... some of the hostas, that when originally planted at our last house were used by Lady and Travis as a bed... and so on. Replanting gifts and memories and sentiments... creating a yard filled with important personal touches.

The irises and hostas have done very well, which would surprise absolutely not one person familiar with such plants. But these two specifically came to mind as Terry and I took a few smaller lilac saplings and moved them. Because quite often, not just when replanted but often for an entire season or two, new locations can provide a bit of a shock. Often the plants don't bloom right away. Give them time though... some nurturing and attention... and they can thrive. We were stunned during our first summer when we the iris and hosta appeared at a level one would consider full strength, and I was wondering how the lilacs would do.

It was three years ago when Terry and I began a process that essentially became a permanent change of address. We moved.

Have you ever moved? And not some five minutes away, still using the same grocery stores, having coffee with mom and dad every day move. I mean needing directions, maps and maybe even a GPS to find the address move. A learning all of the nearby streets, finding new restaurants, figuring out the best places to shop move.

We have.

This time a few hundred miles and into a new state.

Some of the places we frequented in the beginning are ones we no longer visit. Some of the places we enjoyed early on remain favorites for us, and have even become musts for guests when they visit. And we've added several new stops and hangouts and suppliers along the way to today. We've been nurtured by friends, and attentive to details, and we love our new home.

Change can upset things. Not for any reason that is good or bad, but just because change means different.

For a plant, it can mean a bit less sun and a bit less water, for no reasons more complicated than the posts of a fence and the way a gutter directs the rainwater away from the house. And it can mean differences for far more complicated reasons as well.

For a person, it can mean a longer commute, different fresh produce, and the inability to locate anything representing even passable Chinese food.

(Ok… that just got a tad bit specific… but it's also true. There seems to be nothing resembling even so-so Chinese food within a two-hour radius of our new place of residence. Good with the bad… sweet with the sour… and I'd better stop before I talk myself into needing crab rangoon and more, which means a trip to the store so I can make for us.)

The point is, there are shocks to the system. Some small and ordinary, some major and needing action. And relocating… plants and people… create a fairly decent point for comparison. It takes a while to adjust and, so to speak, bloom.

But when you get it right… and everything is in place… the results can be wonderful.

I shouldn't be alive today

A conversation was taking place at work about the differences between today's youth and the kids of my generation (and earlier). I know you'll be stunned to hear this... but most of the people thought that the kids of today are whiney pussies. (I'd put that in quotes, but the actual quote isn't quite as friendly. This pretty much captures the sentiment. And it's worth noting that the feeling expressed went beyond the inability of the newest generation to walk to school, in a blinding rain, uphill... both ways.)

(I'll pause here for a moment so you can fully absorb this stunning news.)

The more you think about it though, the more you understand that beyond the funny name-calling aspects of it, there is definitely something to the claim. The biggest example I'll bring to you involves general health. Have you heard about the studies and articles and theories about how the youth of today are more likely to have problems with allergies, illnesses and all sorts of maladies because they don't eat dirt? Or... more precisely... because everything is so clean, the slightest presence of a germ sends their health into a tailspin?

Let's think about water as an example.

When I was younger and played outside, there was no such thing as bottled water. Not in the current sense of the concept. We drank from the hose... the same hose we had just picked up off of the ground... the same hose we chided one friend for putting his lips against... used for filling the pool and watering the garden... and laughed when the neighborhood dog arrived and took his turn in line.

Oh sure... when we biked over to the park to play tennis, occasionally one of us would be smart enough to fill a thermos with water or lemonade or whatever. But if we wiped the edge of it between drinks and passing it around, it was usually with our sweaty t-shirts.

Long story short... we weren't carrying individual water bottles. We were kids playing and having fun.

And I don't see that today.

Maybe it's computers and video games... kids playing inside instead of in the neighborhood. Maybe it's not. But it sure seems like everyone assembling for massive rounds of hide and go seek has hidden and gone away.

On a universal scale, I believe most of it is a generational thing and the differences are pretty slight. For instance...

I can go to my old home right now and get my father, blindfold him, and bring him to any baseball field in the city I grew up in... which happens to be the same city he grew up in. Then, I could bring him from the car to within fifteen feet of the concession stand. And... I guarantee you... that with ten minutes of taking the blindfold off, he will have found at least one person he knows personally, two people that are related to people he went to school with, and, depending on which of the city high school teams is playing, probably be able to identify at least four players on the field by name.

In short... he knows his community.

The other day Terry, Justin and I stopped in a restaurant. As a waiter approached the table, it turned out Justin knew him. They started casually exchanging a few names... catching up on who was where and doing what.

Not quite the same as identifying people 40 years down the road, but the general concept holds true. Ghost in the graveyard... day long pick-up games of baseball in a cul de sac... whatever... even if Justin didn't have these neighborhood moments, he too knows something of his community. He has been out in the world. And in several ways... I suppose... he has found the hose on the ground for a drink or two on a summer day.

Maybe. Figuratively, if not literally.

My point there being that generations differ in what kinds of events and experiences they provide. And sheltered is not the specific term I'd choose to use in saying that the kids of today are... as previously established... whiney pussies. That evidence has to come from someplace else.

So, what is it?

I never wore a helmet while riding a bike. And I rode it all over the place. No ride to soccer practice? A new album I wanted, but the parents not around to take me to the store? A friend calling and no other way to get to his house? Grab the bike and off I went...

Depending on where you look, you'll find that seat belts in cars become a pattern roughly around 1958 – 1960. It would be a few years later before they become common, and a few years after that for them to catch on as standard items for the rear seats. Effectively, that makes my generation the first born with seat belts in automobiles. My how the times have changed.

And while I may look at safety helmets while riding a bike in the neighborhood as wrong... just wrong... the seatbelt issue is probably a better example of how safety equipment and protecting children has improved over the years.

See the reality is... even if I want to believe that kids today have it easier... with their computers and their toys and their lack of two-mile hikes to and from school... I'm wondering if it's really just me, and my generation, needing to think of them as weaker and untested. We all want more for our kids... while hoping they face less pain as they get it.

Perhaps the kids of today could use a bit more dirt in their diet. And perhaps they could use more responsibility and more accountability around the house. But the fact that they have it easier is a credit to those that came before. And those things we encountered and survived... years of bike riding without a helmet... may or may not be important when considering how easy these kids really have it.

GPS doesn't apply to life

I've been wondering a bit about patterns and habits and so on.

You've quite likely often heard it said that we are creatures of habit. That we repeatedly do things the same way. That we have preferences about things. That patterns do exist, and predictions are not always as mysterious and amazing as they seem.

We drive the same routes to get to work... to see friends... to run errands.

Errands? We spend the majority of our movements stopping at the same grocery store, same gas station, and same restaurants.

We sit in the same chairs around the house. Likely mow the lawn the same way each week... even on the same day of the week.

There's more, but you see the general idea. Some of it may be a result of a work schedule... hard to mow the lawn on a different day when you're not home. Some of it may not be perfect... a sale gets you to a different market, an empty gas tank gets you to a different gas station. And we may have a huge set of rationalizations or reasons for why we do what we do.

We are creatures of habits though. With preferences. Following patterns.

I used to live in a house my GPS hated. Drove it nuts. Kind of.

The fastest way home from places routinely involved this one particular stoplight and a turn to the left. Veronica—the name I've given my GPS—never wanted to turn left.

For whatever reason, Veronica was programmed in such a way that the left turn wasn't an option. It wanted me to go straight through the light, make a u-turn about a half-mile further along the road, come back to the intersection and then turn to the right.

I'm pretty comfortable with the streets around my house. In fact, for that particular intersection, I had been navigating the drive home using it for about seven years before we purchased our first GPS unit. When it came to that intersection... that left-hand turn... I was familiar with it.

Funny thing though, those GPS units. See, that extra half-mile u-turn route it mapped out added a bit of time to the expected journey. With settings designed to give me the fastest available route, every once in a while, those few extra minutes the GPS was adding mattered to the advice the GPS offered. Veronica would advise me to get off the highway at a different exit... routes would be provided with a different turn or approach... and, if you've been paying attention to this little essay, you now understand that Veronica would suggest things that were most certainly not my habits or preferences.

At some point, though I don't recall the specific time it occurred to me, I realized that it was possible this "no left go straight make a u-turn and then come back for a right instead" direction to the house misfire was quite likely not a one-time error for my GPS. Chances weren't just good that there were others, the reality was it would be a miracle of ridiculous odds for that intersection to be the only one in the programming of my GPS with a mistake.

All of which led me to what I found to be an interesting conclusion: How many times have I not been heading home, or driving roads I was familiar with, and I actually took the advice of the GPS? Chances were quite good that on more than one occasion, with me blissfully unaware of it, I had driven a few extra blocks and still arrived at my ultimate destination.

This isn't necessarily about smelling the roses, appreciating the journey, changing things up from time to time, or any other possible cliché or observation that would seem potentially nice and neat and ribbon on the package lovely. I'm not truly debating the ideas of what you know as opposed to what you don't. But since the concept of clichés has been brought up...

I believe we are aware of the idea that most things in life, in order to be valued and experienced, should be viewed as journeys and not destinations. We all want to get to where we are going, but the memories and experiences and thrills are usually found along the way, not always in the arrival. Fair enough.

Often, the journey of life doesn't come with roadside assistance or some navigational tool. We may know right from wrong, and when to do certain things (and when not to). But those times when we want to turn left... know we should turn left... occasionally come with instructions being provided that tell us to go straight. And every so often when we follow the path set out before us, we could be happily rolling along forward when a left also would take us where we want to be.

Yes. I am aware that it's a bit of a stretch. Yes. I am aware of the flowers in bloom that I could see if I simply slowed down a bit while writing this and took a moment to observe them. Perspective matters. But I think the overall idea comes back around and holds true.

For better times and wasted minutes, we are creatures of habit. Instincts and experience will provide us lessons and assistance when we are smart enough to apply them. The prevailing wisdom is not always correct. While we may not always recognize what we are doing or why we are doing it, it very well could be more of an adventure because we didn't. And adventures are not always a bad thing.

A generation gap... of just one year

Many years ago, I was working in a hospital. One of my co-workers was a good friend, and also a year younger than me.

The place isn't important. Neither are the job duties. Instead it's that age difference.

Where we worked, there was just about always a radio playing. The usual setting, as you might expect, was kind of a classic oldies station. Local. Some news. Some weather. And plenty of those great songs you grew up with. Even for the songs you don't consider favorites, the lyrics are etched in the stone of your memory.

One day, my friend and I were walking into the area, and Herman's Hermits was playing. I called out to one of the ladies we worked with.

"Second verse. Same as the first."

"You know it, Bobby," Paula responded.

"What the heck are you two talking about?"
asked Troy.

"The song," I answered. *"'Henry the VIII, I Am' by Herman's Hermits."*

"Henry who?"

It was at that very moment that I realized a line had been drawn. There was a generation gap involving those younger than me.

Paula and I tried to explain to Troy that the song was about a widow that kept marrying guys with the same name. Our efforts didn't go well. He used that to head off into a conversation about how I always ended up dating girls with the same first name. (Which was, at that time, true. True to a degree accompanied by a blindingly hysterical run of stories. True to a degree that I eventually vowed to never ask out a girl with that name ever again. True to a degree that now, decades later, I still chuckle to internal jokes and comments whenever I'm introduced to anyone with that name. The stories of my unfortunate dating experiences, to this day, remain comedy legend.)

We tried to bring him back around with thoughts about "I'm into Something Good" and "There's a Kind of Hush" and more. Didn't work. Actually, fell apart when another friend of ours, a wonderful lady with that kryptonite of a name, came around a corner and sent Troy right back to the first verse of his second tangent.

We did end up laughing quite a bit that afternoon. The damage though, had been done.

The scary part wasn't really that a generation gap existed between me and those younger. No. That was fine.

The scary part was that the line for the start of that gap had been clearly drawn less than a year after I was born. That part hurt. I thought the gap might be a bit larger.

I'd like to say there's more to the story. Something about being young at heart, even for having an older soul. Something like that, or at least founded on similar nonsense. But it wouldn't be true.

Instead, it was just my gray hair moment. The immediate realization that I had climbed a few steps on the ladder, and had some age under my feet.

At least when it happened, the soundtrack was pretty good.

Tired of soapbox preaching? Take a seat and listen.

There's a problem when people speak. And it's a big one.

You have to consider the source.

Unfortunately: (1) everyone has an opinion, and, (2) everyone tends to view their opinions as if facts.

If you give someone the right stage, the message can carry. Toss in a naïve person or ignorant approach, and suddenly a poorly conceived and vastly flawed opinion takes on a tremendous life as if it's undisputedly solid.

Part of the fun is that we, as a society, tend to hand microphones and soapboxes out based as much for celebrity status as for well-deserved knowledge and experience.

Is that wrong?

Not always. If you'll allow a broad, sweeping concept for the idea of a celebrity, these people can get doors to open, media to pay attention, and projects placed into motion. Celebrities can inspire… celebrities can impress… celebrities can do.

Once again though—another potential brick wall—consider the source.

Let's say you hail from Rhode Island. Two... three... four generations of your family call the state home. You lived there for at least twenty years, and likely more.

Such a pedigree does not automatically equate to a knowledge about the state. It doesn't mean you know dozens of recipes that use coffee syrup, have immediate recall of the locations and operating hours of at least three diners serving hot wieners, or have a passionate preference on whether or not celery is appropriate when making lobster salad.

Such a pedigree does not combine with a driver's license from the State of Rhode Island and Providence Plantations to create the ability to handle a motor vehicle in snow and ice.

Being a celebrity might get a person through a door that was otherwise closed. Being a celebrity might create an aura that immediately settles around a room when you enter. Being a celebrity does not make you an authority on... well... on anything.

Still... consider the value. Often the biggest hurdle in any process is getting an audience. Celebrity... through door with eyes turned. Unknown and unrecognized expert... outside looking in, with no one noticing.

I will grant you, all too often hearing what people decide to share when they get on the soapbox can be frightening. At times unprepared, at times ignorant, the reality is the spotlight does not create brilliant observations. That doesn't mean there's nothing worth hearing.

An idea that I've shared at times before: Always hear the other side.

I was in college, taking a class in Constitutional Law. The professor preached those five words. Always hear the other side.

The biggest part of the advice was simply getting an understanding of the material you aren't bringing to the table. Once you had that information, you could then apply it however you saw fit. You could feel even more secure in your position or adjust your argument, and you could always disregard the other thoughts and cast them aside.

One naïve or entitlement driven piece of stupidity does not mean that all opinions, causes, ideas and more are wrong or without merit. But...

The problem honestly isn't always with the idiots on the soapbox. Far too many times, it's with the audience. Blindly following or quickly objecting, often with no thought given to what is actually being said.

The next time someone is getting attention based on their name... or position... or any other reason beyond actual experience and knowledge, take a moment to listen to what they have to say. Don't judge. Don't get angry. Just listen.

And then... for the idiots... walk away, because you've given them enough.

Once in a while though, you might learn something you never would have heard with political correctness or predetermined conclusions clouding the message.

Go Fish

Ever wonder where some of our traditional games come from?

Go Fish.

That's a good one. Such a classic that we've all heard the expression. And, in the true sense of the game, that's pretty much exactly what you are doing. Fishing. You toss the question out there... the bait... and hope for a hit. Later, that bait can work against you, since you're casting out the information that you have that rank of card in your hand.

The term "go fish" has come to refer to something that is almost a hopeless and lost cause. You're off on a fishing expedition... gone fishing. It might be the sarcastic response given when you don't get what you ask for. And how about those legendary fishing tales? Kind of works there too.

It doesn't appear that the game ever had anything to do with fishing though. At least not until one variation of the game became more noted and popular.

August Smith is credited with the first documented version of the game. But it wasn't called Go Fish at the time. He created a game called Authors. Produced by a company called Whipple & Smith, I suppose given the name that it wouldn't surprise you to learn that it involved matching up famous authors. Most of what I found looking it up appears at times closer to a flip memory game than a deck of cards in hand, but the foundations have connections.

And from a bit of research… that history line leads us back even further…

The game of Authors is traced back to other origins, possibly even back to the Middle Ages. Before settling in with August Smith, we should probably head over to Europe and a game called Quartet. Based around similar player actions, this is a German version of the game. And it is actually believed that Authors may have been taken from Quartet.

There is a British version of the game is known as Happy Families, and as you can plainly see, with a bit of looking around we are finding several games… different places and regions… many claiming to be the original… and no way to confirm degrees of initial design, coincidence, inspiration and more. Authors may be a reproduction of a previous game, and simply fortunate enough to be the first one documented.

The reason it is called Go Fish for so many of us today would likely be the ever fun and basic results of popularity. Funny thing those copyright laws. International laws didn't exist in the middle years of the 1800s. They came about around 1890. So, even if we do give our nod to Authors as the source, it was reproduced in many forms but no one is going to be able to fight for credit. Go Fish wins.

Want to get silly anyway? Authors eventually branched out in to other categories, such as Inventors and Presidents. And the number of cards dealt differs, depending on the game being played, and perhaps more importantly, the deck being used.

History can be a fascinating journey. For most of us though, all that really matters is whether or not you have any sevens.

Everything is bad for you... but this takes the cake

It's been a strange week. That's true for many reasons, but for now we'll focus on something I posted about recently, which was that a new study showed that regularly drinking diet soda can significantly increase your chances of having a stroke or heart attack.

Of course, that announcement has quickly been met by all sorts of side stories, opposing viewpoints, and a fair amount of attention. And honestly... in the stories I've read they say not to jump to any conclusions. More time and research is needed to prove this is any sort of definitive and accurate understanding.

If you've been coming to the Backpack for a while, you know how I can be at times. When studies say drink more water... say again drink more water... assert it's great, no calories, your body needs it... say again drink more water... only to follow a year or so later with an announcement that people are overhydrating... well, I laugh.

When testing shows that water—even bottled water—may have been touched by waste and runoff so that it's tainted with drugs... well, I roll my eyes.

In many cases my reactions are based on wondering what the heck the people are thinking with their research and announcements. Perhaps the results just seem so blazingly obvious... perhaps the work seems like such a waste of time... perhaps the findings are so far off where one would think shocking... why... why... why?

It just seems so much simpler and more acceptable to me to look for a middle ground where there are elements of the issue that we can all agree about. In the case of the environment, we could easily say that we treat the planet horrendously instead of worrying about whether or not someone believes in global warming, need to examine ways of recycling and participate in such programs, and overall just need to be more aware of how we act and what we do. Not many people can argue with that rationally... and no polar bears need to be branded or trademarked or brought into the discussion.

Should we stop littering and use our resources better? Yes. (End of discussion... let's get to work.)

Why do I mention all of this and recent news? Well... here we go...

A study from Cornell says that working mothers could be one of the causes of overweight kids.

(I know. I know. But hold on. It gets crazier.)

Another study says that exposing infants to solid foods earlier may be linked to weight problems.

And... yeah.

Ok... let's approach this from a different path...

Do you really need me... or your doctor... or some Ivy League study... to tell you that a diet consisting only of cookies, chocolate pudding and grape soda isn't healthy?

Would you be stunned if I suggested to you that by getting some exercise and eating sensibly, you'll feel a bit better?

(Eat right and exercise may not be perfect or complete as a health plan, but as opposed to eating nothing but marshmallows and watching fourteen hours of television daily I think it stands on some secure ground. And so…)

Working mothers? Ok. How many families can survive long term with only one parent working? Did the study take into account single-parent homes? What if a grandparent lived in the home and was there for childcare and supervision?

Did any of these factors (or others) become considerations, and if so, did they change the results? I don't know… and evidently, they don't either. The article I read said that a father's occupation, divorce, and other potential factors couldn't be accounted for. Not kidding. They couldn't make conclusions for many factors that could be involved and might alter the basic conclusion. Heck, apparently they couldn't even account for scenarios such as whether or not the parents worked at the same time, had overlapping schedules, or always had at least one of them available to be home.

I ask you… given that studies are making claims that they can't provide answers about… are we really that far away from seeing a study that says a household with a man and a woman, with only the man working, two-point-three kids, a dog and a fence, is the healthiest way to grow up? (Don't laugh. I'll bet I could find something that says pretty much exactly that in five internet searches or less.)

There are questions to be asked of any results. For example (and this is a really good one): Who funded the study? It's often amazing when you see a claim and learn that the answers fall right in line, step for step, with the beliefs of the individual or company that gave the dollars to conduct the research.

Could a group advocating stay at home moms or breastfeeding be behind these studies I'm noting? Don't know… but it's certainly possible.

And even if there isn't something sneaky taking place… for me, once again, it becomes a question of responsibility. If I slump into the chair with a glass of milk and a slice of cake instead of taking a walk and eating an apple, I can't blame anyone but myself when I gain a couple of pounds.

And how about the research conditions and longevity. Those overweight babies eating solid foods? Article I read said they had been tracked for a whopping total of three years. Yup. According to the article, that's true. In other words, they are claiming that babies place on solid foods before they are four months of age are more likely to be overweight around their third birthday. Not when the reach school age… not as teenagers… not overweight for life.

As always though… perhaps it's just me.

Maybe I don't know enough about these studies. Maybe I'm missing the point.

What I do know is that the results are being presented and reported by mass media outlets as if the information within pertains to us all. The blurbs and quotes are made more generic and shocking to get us to read the articles… and maybe buy the products of some sponsors.

Regularly drinking diet soda may be bad for you.

Is this really a surprising concept? I suppose if you live in a household with a working mother or eat solid foods, you might want to check that out.

The fact of a brownie

Allow me to start this article with a thought that first came to me about twenty years ago or so...

One understood part of eating a brownie is that you are cheating. The sugar, the chocolate, the sinfully-fudgy-goodness. While it certainly doesn't qualify as health food by a list of ingredients, the joy of eating one is without question good for you. And the experience is almost exclusively based on it being so good because it is so bad.

Back then, I came to this conclusion about brownies because I had begun to be aware of low-fat foods appearing in the stores and in commercials. And I didn't understand. When I ate a brownie, I was most certainly not thinking about a diet. Salads and smaller portions were the important consideration for diets in my childhood mind. The fact of a brownie was its sinfully-fudgy-goodness. Take that away, make it low-fat, and what's the point of eating it at all?

Within that concept is where you could find my approach to low-fat foods, no sugar added offerings, and almost all diet handbooks. And now a new fad... and yes, it is a fad... nothing more and with little lasting credibility in my mind... has taken over the country. That fad is low carb.

I will admit that my thoughts about brownies became a lasting part of my approach to food back when diets consisted of eating cottage cheese with pineapple chunks, or subsisting solely on carrots or grapefruit for weeks. I am firmly convinced that we have plain cottage cheese and pineapple diets of just three decades ago to thank for all of the flavored cottage cheese, cream cheese, and other assorted items located near the yogurt in the store today. Someone lived on it for a diet, appreciated that the world deserved better, and created it.

Along those same lines, I do appreciate that diet food has improved over the years. Some of it even tastes pretty darn good. Perhaps... just perhaps... a fad or two might even race past being a trend and become a lasting belief.

But the fact of a brownie remains. And here's what I mean...

I've written before about how the four food groups of my youth have disappeared. I've also made notes about how everything is bad for you now. Without going too deeply into them, here are the classic four... diary, breads and grains, meats, and fruits and vegetables.

Dairy – Milk or no milk? Good or bad? Whole, skim, 1% or 2 %? What level is good? What level is bad?

Breads and grains – Bread? You aren't really going to eat bread are you?

Meats – Red meat isn't good for you.

Fruits and vegetables – The last of those four basic food groups to fall... but I swear that as just one thought, I have seen that as you begin to diet many fruits are bad for you because they can actually make you feel hungry quite soon after eating them.

In any event, everything that I was told to focus on as a child has, by one organization or another, been declared bad for me. In fact, the entire four food groups have been replaced by a pyramid and commercials with baseball legend Ozzie Smith telling me to eat just nine... *nine*... servings of fruits and vegetables a day.

Wow.

Funny thing is, I have never heard anyone debate the old advice of eating right and exercising. What is eating right is open to debate... but still. Smaller portions, not as many desserts, take a walk. Not a bad plan at all.

I admit I'm tired of all the Atkins, South Beach, and so on diets all over the place. As topics, they will disappear or be updated as time moves on. New and improved editions of books to sell. Cottage cheese replaced by Stairmasters replaced by drinking water replaced by Atkins replaced by South Beach. And then, I heard about a new product a few weeks ago, and years of treating claims as background noise were overwhelmed.

Low carb Coca-Cola.

You have to be kidding me.

Low carb Coca-Cola?

Please, it can't be... but it could be.

Low carb Coca-Cola... with low carb Pepsi on the way.

We've officially gone too far. Way, way, *way* too far.

When I was younger I used to watch *The Jetsons* on television, and I couldn't wait to have a system in the house for ordering food like they did. Walk up, tell it what I wanted, and poof, there was dinner. A microwave oven came close to the reality, but it wasn't the same. To be honest, as things move forward, I'm not so sure that twenty-years from now the healthy people won't be eating anything but saw dust. Of course, not pressure-treated saw dust. That would be bad. And yet that sure seems like where we are heading. Sawdust and a water... with lemon.

Too much water is bad for you. Read that this past year. And now my carbonated beverages are worried about losing their markets because of carbs.

Deep... deep... *deep* breath. Sigh.

It's all too much for me. Maybe they won't be eating saw dust in twenty-years, but I can guarantee you one thing... all these foods people are telling us are good today won't be part of the approved diets tomorrow.

And now I need a brownie.

The Big Sky

I've always known Montana as the "Big Sky" state. And I've never been completely certain of why that is.

I can guess. (And I'm sure my guesses would add up to a fairly accurate portrayal.)

The natural scenery, in any and all pictures I've seen, is stunning. Breathtaking. Easily the kind of beauty that—when surrounded by it—creates a sadness any time you need to go inside.

The state may have some cities you may know by name, it most definitely does not have cities you know by skyscraper heights. In fact, without looking it up, I'd bet Rhode Island has at least one building taller than any in Montana.

And what do you get when you add outdoor splendor with no tall structures? Sure... an exceptional view of the sky. Big sky. Makes sense.

(Since I was writing this, I looked it up. In two sources I checked, there was uniform agreement (so I stopped at two). Just the city of Providence, Rhode Island, has six buildings listed that are taller than any throughout the entire state of Montana. More than two dozen buildings in New England are taller than the top building in Providence. Montana skylines are not obstructed by tall buildings.)

The trick is, more often than not when the nickname and Montana come up, I don't have any resources handy for looking at background about the nickname. For most of my life, I was stuck living in New England—Rhode Island and Connecticut—and despite my travels, had never been overwhelmed by a big sky type feeling.

You kind of hear "big sky", nod your head, and move along.

That has since changed for me.

In New York.

My wife and I moved to upstate New York fairly recently. Our house is less than three decades old, built along a stretch where I am fairly certain most of the houses occupy land previously used for growing corn and such.

I can't prove that corn idea, but I can say everyone has about an acre or more of property around their house, and the trees nearby do not possess the appearance (or height) that would suggest the applicable possibility of any definition of old growth. It would be fair (and just about right) to say that you could look in one direction at the horizon line formed by earth/sky, turn 180-degrees, and look at another horizon line of earth/sky. (Not accurate... a handful of trees... a few swells and hills... but no numerous towering oaks, massive mountains, or cloud-touching Superman Buildings. Earth. Sky. A view of where they meet. (Superman Building. Another Rhode Island joke.))

Quite often I find myself outside, in the yard or sitting on the deck, perhaps enjoying a gorgeous sunset. Many times, I head out to be swept away by the stargazing opportunities. And it is staggering.

Big sky.

No... wait... BIG sky.

I have had the pleasure of a variety of travels in my life. I've seen sunsets in multiple countries. Sunrises too. Been witness to some sensational wonders of nature. For whatever reason though, until I was in this backyard, I can't say that "big sky" ever came to mind.

It is a beautiful sight.

There's something spellbinding about a clear midnight sky. And big sky overnight? It can look huge. Beyond huge. When you truly get away from civilization, when the eyes adjust and no other lights are around, and you see that blanket of stars overhead...

Wow. Just wow.

I understand Big Sky now. And I have no doubts that Montana—unofficial or not—is deserving of their claim. Still, as I write this, we've had a wonderful day around here. The sun is going down. And I do believe I am going to head outside and enjoy the view.

Might even stay in a comfortable chair until late in the evening. Watch as the sky stretches out pretty much forever. Should be pretty close to perfect.

I gat suit correct

…and I do… I so honestly and completely do.

Now, don't get me wrong… for all the gat I feel, the reality is that suit correct is something that has worked in my favor, and likely benefitted me significantly more often than it has frustrated me. You might say I love suit correct.

But honestly… those times when it doesn't help out… it tends to make me look like an idiot far more often than could be seen as amusing.

One day a few weeks ago I was sending a text message to a friend… autocorrect updated something, and it updated it in a spectacularly idiotic fashion. Like many of you, I'm sure, I noticed the error after hitting send, and immediately decided to follow up with a simple message…

"*I hate autocorrect*"

Which in turn I typed too quickly and it was corrected, and just like that I sent along…

"I gat suit correct"

What?

No. Really. What?

Now we could begin with a long tirade here that continues piling on to autocorrect. But that might be too easy. So... let's check out the alternative it provided. Because, for me the frustrating part is how often the corrections completely ignore my original intentions.

Do you know what gat means?

There are actually a few possibilities.

First up is slang for a gun. I have no desire to shoot any suit of mine, which means we can move right along.

Second is a channel, or some kind of passage, that may occur naturally or artificially. You also might find that this passage definition has something to do with an Old Norse transition from an Old English word for a gate.

Do enough research, and you'll find other things such as references to gat as an older version of the word get.

Where we end up is that apparently—instead of hating autocorrect—in order to fix my suit, I needed to keep moving through the gate. Not exactly my intention.

None of this helps me out when autocorrect goes about fixing a mistake that isn't a mistake... adds or removes apostrophes without any apparent consistency (or accuracy)... and all of the other annoying habits of the process.

It also doesn't help that should you even consider turning autocorrect off, the errors that are likely to begin slipping through an Old Norse passageway into your text and email content will explode in frequency quite likely beyond your imagination.

And so, it's a trade I make... the corrections I see happening that I'm thankful took place outweigh the frustrations of the suit correct I gat so much.   And it's probably a trade you willingly make as well.

Signs of an e-mail scheme

Today I want to take a few minutes to cover what has become, for me, an increasingly interesting and scary part of our collective feelings about technology.

Essentially… we're much too casual and trusting.

But, I think you may already know that. And, I think you may already be aware of the concept on which I plan to base things.

I'd like to believe that… even if we can't all recognize them… all of us are at least aware of things like scams, schemes, viruses and other computer issues and woes. I'm not saying all of us can spot them. I'm not saying any of us can recognize all of them. I'm not even saying we are good at handling them. Instead, while we might not all know the specifics about the fund transfer con where a prince promises millions of dollars tomorrow for assistance by providing hundreds today, I am saying I feel comfortable believing we are all aware that scams exist.

But every few weeks... no, actually, every few hours... I see the signs that people don't seem to think much of the threats associated with scams and viruses and more.

This worries me.

For a moment though, let's step away from e-mail and yet still consider technology. Have you ever used a GPS?

While the stories have become legendary (and in some cases a bit beyond far-fetched), the realities are simple: people are driven to place blame in any direction except toward personal responsibility. People claim they were misled, directed to become lost, often in well-beyond-frequented-roads locations... phantom left and right turns, into woods and waters... and yet on and on, it's the GPS at fault.

So many places around the internet... so many smartphones and apps... so many pieces of technology... want to know who we know. Requests are made for contacts and e-mail addresses and more. Network, network, network. Connect, connect, connect.

Log on to Facebook and Twitter and other social media sites. Within moments you'll likely see something that causes you to chuckle or your eyes to roll.

And yet, to an extent, none of this should be interpreted as a belief that people are ignorant. GPS units do make mistakes... there are benefits to sharing information and joining together... group interactions and expressions do not have to be serious and perfect and formed around your opinions and preferences.

Which brings us back to awareness (and ultimately to those e-mail schemes). I never meant to literally offer up a list featuring the top five or so signs for recognizing a scam in your inbox. Instead... consider...

Knowing and recognizing your surroundings (literally and figuratively) matters. It's a key part of taking directions, sharing information, and mingling with the world.

You know how silly and stupid some of those scams seem? Misspelled words or hideous phrasing... few details or specifics in the message... and all sorts of items that seem like sure signs of no good in progress. Did it ever occur to you that much of that could be intentional?

Sure, 99% of people... if not more (though likely less)... will hit delete immediately. Gone. But that 1%.

If you are actually someone that doesn't catch those errors or tipoffs, chances are good you'll be typing in personal information or clicking on those links. Odds are also good that embarrassment will kick in, and you won't be looking to report the problem quickly. Simply put...

Target the gullible, experience less problems.

Is there a line? ...a simple answer? No. Of course not. A solution to one issue is often seen as just a challenge to adjust the rules and play again. But there is awareness.

I believe that there is a difference between taking a wrong turn and driving into a lake. If your GPS doesn't get you to your destination, or adds miles to your trip, that is a problem though it may not be beyond explanation. Drive your car across the beach and into the ocean because the GPS said go, and honestly, you really should be watching your surroundings and attempting to operate the vehicle safely.

Pay attention. That's all. You don't need to approach everything as if it's evil... but you do need to understand that it could be.

Talking to myself

I find I'm talking to myself more now than ever.

I'm not sure what to make of that.

It's not quite Walter Mitty stuff mind you. I'm not pitching for the Orioles or quarterbacking the Buccaneers. I haven't been strutting across a stage... in some strange reenactment of a scene from *Risky Business*... belting out songs from my latest CD.

I have been quoting excerpts from my soon-to-be-(oh-don't-I-wish) best seller. Maybe that deserves a bit of explanation.

I find I always do my best writing, unfortunately for both you and me, when I am far away from pen, paper or computer. It generally takes place when I am walking with my dogs, when I'm in the shower, or when I'm driving my car. Things like that. So, when I participated recently in National Novel Writing Month, I spent lots of time talking out loud, to myself, about sections that I wanted to write. Very rarely did the words on paper reach the level of quality

I believe I achieved when cruising along on the highway. I should also point out that my dogs didn't offer as much critical support as I had hoped for.

But for some reason, even having spent so much time writing a draft of a novel during the month of November, I find myself wondering if I am talking to myself too much.

When I was younger... much, much younger... I used to love the Creature Double-Feature on television. One of my favorite movies was *Voyage into Space*. It was a tale about Giant Robot and the child that controlled him. Without going into too much detail, let's just say that I spent plenty of time staring out the elementary school window while whispering into my watch.

There are people out there that will understand what I mean... I know... I checked out Giant Robot, *Voyage into Space*, and Johnny Sokko on the internet. Plenty of us were staring out windows, our wrists raised to our lips, and our eyes focused on the horizon hoping for a flying robot to streak into view.

But things are different today. People tell you strange things when they catch you talking to yourself. "As long as you aren't answering yourself," is one great response. Or how about "are the voices in there friendly?" I don't get much comfort from that one.

I suppose I shouldn't be too concerned. Just as long as I don't wind up seeing this article in the hands of my wife's lawyer I'll be fine. And, in case for some reason my wife does find need for a lawyer, how about if we say that the voices I hear in my head... the conversations I have with myself... normally include the following:

"I should probably mow the lawn today."

"There are four different kinds of orange juice for each brand. I don't know what brand she drinks, forget about remembering pulp, no pulp, or calcium added!"

*"Oh shoot (*only I don't say shoot*), it's trash night."*

Usually though you'll find me combining them all together... I grab my car keys because I need to go to the store. Walking out to the car I see the trash can and remember that the pick-up is tomorrow. So, I bring the bags to the curb before getting in the car. The conversation along this entire walk goes something like: "Milk, juice and a vegetable for dinner. Milk, juice and a vegetable for dinner. Milk, juice and... oh shoot, trash day. Guess I'll bring this stuff out now. Oh, looks like the grass needs to be mowed. Has it been over a week already? I don't think it's supposed to rain tomorrow. Guess I'll get it then. Ok, milk, bread and... umm... juice. Juice. Does she like it with or without pulp? I guess I could get both. Wait, do I like it with or without pulp? If I don't like it I'm not drinking it just because she didn't like it but I bought it."

And the conversation goes happily along that path until I return home, walk in the house, unpack the groceries and get asked...

"Did you forget the vegetables?"

Yes. I did.

I wonder how she puts up with me? Probably because I usually add ice cream to the list of things I did get.

In any event I don't think I'm all that close to walking down the street, no one within twenty feet of me, fists clinched, teeth locked in a grimace, and under my breath forcefully arguing "next time *get your own* orange juice."

I guess I'm not tremendously concerned.

For now.

Could someone PLEASE answer the phone

Here we go... pet peeve time.

I cannot stand answering the phone to find a computer speaking to me in a way suggesting that I should be grateful for the call while offering nothing that even slightly interests me.

Companies want my business, but they don't want to talk to me. I'm not worth their time. I'm not worth their investment.

At all.

They don't want to answer my questions. They don't want to hear my complaints. They don't want to know if I'm having a nice day. All of which makes a bit of sense, since I don't want to talk to anyone that's frustrated, disappointed, and potentially upset with me, and I rarely enjoy discussing the weather with someone I don't know that well.

When my phone rings... when they are approaching me... when they want my money... yeah, that prerecorded happy-tone-as-if-smiling voice is insulting.

This is not a swipe at technology.

In general, I actually understand automated systems and networks and programming. I don't necessarily like them most of the time. And I definitely don't enjoy having to spin around three times tapping my nose while rubbing my belly before falling to my knees with hope against hope that I have produced the right sequence of events and now might pick the right number to connect me to a representative since nothing from their side ever explained how to connect with a representative.

I've also gotten used to people and places and things and more that don't want to be contacted. No telephone numbers, no e-mail addresses, no fancy forms to fill out before proving I'm not a robot and clicking send listed at all.

Actually, there are occasionally times that I need to do something and don't want to talk to them. Checking a payment status for instance. So, it works both ways. Some times.

And then, there it goes again—phone ringing—and if I decide to answer the call, it's not a person. There's a voice though. Looking for business.

Ugh.

Not all phone calls without a person are bad. Not all of them annoy me. For instance, when I get a reminder from a doctor about an upcoming appointment. There's a purpose there. And an understanding of efficiency. I gave the office a certain phone number to contact me, they are reaching out to let me know I'm expected in a day or two, and all of us benefit from the process. That works.

My pet peeve... my problem... is when I answer the phone and the business on the other side can't be bothered to speak with me. Yet, I should be grateful. It's in the tone of the recorded voice. Bubbly and happy and for all the world sounding like they work for the greatest company in the world while prepping me for the sales pitch. It's a tone that suggests the purpose of the call is to do me a personal and great favor.

Yeah... no.

My internet and television and telephone services are just fine not bundled. I don't need fifteen seconds of how great your service is and how I can benefit from a year of combining them for just $29.95. I most certainly will not call the 1-800 number, hang on the line, or press 1 now to hear more about new windows for my home. If you couldn't be bothered having a representative call me directly from the start to discuss roofing or fencing or whatever, then I don't need to listen to some music while waiting to speak with the next available representative. And I definitely do not feel as though my call is important to you (especially when I didn't make it).

As with anything, the answers are found in money. Programming can be set up so the same message gets played thousands and thousands of times during business hours (as if there are any true business hours any more, since they seem to call whenever these days). No breaks needed for the recorded voice for lunch or the restroom. No medical benefits provided for the recorded voice doing all the work.

Savings... savings... savings... and, perhaps, one or two people actually will write down the number to call later, wait through the music, or press 1. Perhaps, one or two people actually will make a purchase or look for more information.

It just won't be me.

Water repellant towels

If Terry and I could isolate our occasional heated moments into one example, it would be towels.

Specifically, these moments involve what I call water repellant towels.

(The fact that I'm saying an example of heated moments would involve towels should tell you things are pretty good between the two of us. And when it comes to the description of the towels, some of you are nodding your heads with understanding and sympathy already. For those that aren't... a water repellant towel is one that doesn't absorb any water. At all. When you use a water repellant towel, you basically just spread water around.)

Terry has a habit of buying water repellant towels. And then, when I notice, she has the nerve to try and use one of two excuses as her defense against my complaints.

The first excuse is that once washed a few times, the towels will be fine. And this is just a flat out lie. The strange thing though, is that I don't mind this one. It's an attempt to get me to be quiet. I get it. But the reality of the situation is simple... for a few runs through the laundry, the lint filter gets quite the workout... when it comes to drying a person off however, the towels—after one trip through the washer or fifty—continue to work about as well as a sheet of Saran Wrap.

The second excuse is the one that troubles me. In this one, the consistent theme is that the purchase was a smart one, and simply too good to pass up. Terry tries defending her actions because they look so lovely. Often they match something... a shower curtain, toothbrush holder, or bathmat. Occasionally they were on sale. Once they were an amazing bargain for such a terrific brand.

I'll stop there... because, let's face it... how many of us can actually provide a brand name for quality bath and body towels? And to clarify, I'm not talking about a favorite store. No answering me with: "I like to buy my towels at fill-in-the-blank." A store name is not a brand of towels. I mean that you read the question and said: "Well, there's Artthur Frank. I'll always buy Artthur Frank towels."

(Artthur Frank... I didn't make that up. I hopped on the inter-web-thingy and did a search for "quality towel manufacturer brands" and Artthur Frank was the first response. That's not a spelling error. I can't say that I've ever heard of Artthur Frank before the search engine of choice pointed me in that direction. Can't tell you I'll ever hear of Artthur Frank again. The point remains... few people know the best names in towels, and even fewer have a need for such knowledge. Now back to the story...)

My problem could be even more detailed, but we've shared enough to get to the main troubles. And I'll move over to that with a question...

How many different ways can you decorate your bathroom? I mean, right now. Without leaving your home or apartment. Just what you have available.

Today our bathroom is kind of formal. I guess you could call the decorations neutral colors, mainly browns and beiges, with fancy swirled handles on the accessories and basic but distinct patterns on the shower curtain rings.

That's at this very moment.

In our basement is a container with another bathroom set. Sea turtles and dolphins and greens and blues. Cups and waste baskets and shower curtain rings and—of course— even a few color-coded hand towels that only come out on special occasions.

Next to it is another container with parrots and reds and palm trees and yellows and tropical jungle stuff.

And another with anything you could imagine using for a bathroom in either dusty rose or a color that matches up ever so nicely with dusty rose.

And then another... blues.

And... and you get the idea. Once we get past five possible bathroom themes, they all sort of run together in some way—even providing interchangeable options—and the grand total is no longer important.

Remember excuse number two though? Purchased because they were lovely or matched or whatever?

A smart purchase. You do not pass this buy purchase. Well... just because something works when you have the whales and dolphins and sea turtles out does not mean it matches everything from the dusty rose container.

She claims these towels are bought for many reasons... function and décor... but that's not true either. However, as opposed to being a pants-on-fire moment designed to find a possible momentary end to the debate, this time it's a lie as an attempt to justify the purchase. And that's just insulting.

Let's gingerly tread into the differences of men and women debate for a moment here. (As if, perhaps, I hadn't crossed that road already.)

Terry tends to avoid the larger towels in our linen closet. It has something to do with washing her hair and using multiple smaller bath towels instead of multiple bigger towels.

I am fine with this. It makes sense.

I normally reach for a larger bath towel though. Washing my hair does not necessitate an extra towel. And, I love the days after laundry has been washed and folded because—yeah, you guessed it—all of the best towels are available.

I don't go for the smaller bath towels unless the larger water absorbent ones are gone – she doesn't go for the larger ones unless the smaller ones are gone.

So far, so good.

When the latest shopping has been done though, and the bags are entering the house, guess which style of bath towel Terry has bought? Absolutely – the water repellant towels are just about always the larger size that she rarely uses.

This brings us to a nifty conclusion in the debate. When Terry buys more towels, she tends to buy the larger towels of the style that she doesn't use and that I do, and she buys them in the water repellant style that I absolutely hate.

Somehow, that's my fault.

Which wouldn't be so bad... I can handle the blame, misguided or not. But what generally happens isn't a case of whether or not I should buy my own darn towels. No... what happens is that even she avoids the water repellant ones.

Heck, can you guess what happens to make room for the latest purchases? Sure you can. The good towels—those would be "good" in my opinion, and means the ones that actually absorb water and work like, you know, towels—get removed from the linen closet and end up in some location that I have yet to find. Space is tight... new towels need a home… and suddenly water repellant towels have taken over the house.

With Terry also first using the few water absorbent ones.

(Lovely.)

I probably should have had a destination in mind for this essay when I began. Something more than it being an example of relationships. Perhaps a push to make an item that shows the friendly battles that are created when a house becomes a home.

But the inspiration for it came from a simple moment. This morning I woke up, made my way to the shower, and reached for a towel. The laundry is done, but still in baskets downstairs for now, and I was left wishing for something better than the towels available. Something like Saran Wrap.

What are we missing?

Check out this lyric from a song called "Play for Today" by The Cure:

> *It's not a case of aiming to please*
> *You know you're always crying*
> *It's just your part*
> *in the play for today*

Not bad... and actually, I love the song. Other lyrics from it (which I won't quote here), are fairly typical of Robert Smith... and frankly, brilliant.

A few days ago, I saw an article on the BBC web site. Turns out there are plans to revive a show I never knew existed. The show is called *Play for Today*. And although the name is set to change, the idea is basically the same... a quest for new talent.

Take another look at the last two lines I used from the song...

It's just your part
in the play for today

I would be willing to guarantee you that Smith is quite aware of the existence of the original show (which ran twenty years before wrapping up in 1984). I'm guessing that several people in England have probably put the line and the show together... or that a connection was made at the time of its release... but it isn't something I have been able to find on the internet. It was completely lost on me over the years, and I never would have seen it if I hadn't stumbled across the article announcing the revamped show.

This is something I wonder about all the time. Robin Williams voiced the part of the Genie in Disney's *Aladdin*, and he inserted line after line that went away from the actual script... doing plenty of imitations and voices that were incorporated into the film. For an audience in 1992... and even today... Williams is hysterical and a direct hit. But what about fifty years from now? Will audiences then recognize the characters? Will they get the jokes?

I use that as an explanation to move a step further... and ask you to consider the absolute classic... *Snow White and the Seven Dwarfs*. It stands to reason that there is something in virtually every frame of that movie that we, as an audience almost seventy years removed from its debut, are missing. Perhaps caricatures of certain people. The presence of certain types of furniture. Maybe a rabbit or a bird or a deer happened to be the favorite animal of the daughter of one of the animators drawing a scene of Snow White out in the woods. Maybe that same little girl liked to wear blue and red and yellow.

We don't know. At least, not that I can find in some specific place.

And overall it doesn't change the fact that the movie is outstanding and unique and, for many people, one of the greatest films ever made. A legendary, industry changing production.

As time moves on, and productions get cuter and cuter, things like specific words or items being inserted into songs, books and movies will become easier and easier to overlook and forget. Heck, retail outlets are advertising on the billboards in video games now. But there is an art to some of it. When the staff at Pixar work on the fine print of a newspaper, or the titles of compact discs, or the pictures on a wall in one of their films... that's art. That's hidden meaning.

And although I can't confirm it, I believe the same holds true for the "play for today" line in Smith's song and a connection with the show. It's there. It's something that's fully intended to add depth to the meaning of the line.

The simple question becomes... how often are we missing the true intent when it should be right there in front of us?

Frustration from the dashboard light

I don't want to give the impression that, in my opinion, every vehicle produced by one particular car manufacturer comes with the service engine soon light permanently turned on. But over the past two decades I've owned a few different models from the same car company… and, yes, the service engine soon light was lit on each of the vehicles far more often than it wasn't.

And, like the tire inflation light on one vehicle—yes, same company—those check the engine lights almost without exception appear to be on for no discernible reason whatsoever. That has me worried, since the results from just about every time we've checked in the past essentially revealing no service needed soon, I've become a bit numb to any and all versions of a service engine soon light in any vehicle.

Right up front I want you to know, I am not a mechanic. In fact, it probably would be a miracle if you considered me capable of changing the oil on your older, beat up, don't care if it runs when I'm finished lawn mower. And that's a decision based solely on my being capable of doing it. Ability. Not qualifications. You almost certainly would never consider me qualified to change the oil on a lawn mower.

My joke or statement or however you viewed it, about it being one car manufacturer... it's not a swipe at any specific car manufacturer, even if my findings point toward one. Nor, it might be worth noting, am I honestly saying there is absolutely no reason for these lights to be on. The jokes are because: (1) It just so happens that when I speak with friends that also own cars made by the company, they all seem to have service engine soon light stories. Eerily similar stories. And while owners from other car companies tell me of fun experiences, those are never delivered at such a high percentage. (2) When I have had the lights checked, they never involved any issue where repairs would have made a car run more efficiently, correctly, and whatever concept (or description) you'd like to apply to arrive at proper operation. The cars were running fine. The cars were well taken care of. Service engine soon light came on indicating a repair that would have cost more than one hundred dollars (and usually a few hundred dollars) while doing absolutely nothing for the vehicle's operation and performance levels. I literally could have fixed something such as the handle on the glove compartment and done more for vehicle operation than attending to the needs of the light.

Let's swerve over toward a different dashboard light to explain what I mean about the light is on, but nothing would improve if we fixed what it was saying idea.

One of our cars has that fancy tire pressure warning light. During the first year or two that we had it, the light would often come on in cold weather. The situation played out like this: (1) Get in car on cold morning (temperature below freezing) and begin the drive to work. (2) Travel approximately ten miles (virtually all on a highway), tire pressure light begins flashing. (3) Tire pressure light stops flashing and remains lit for remainder of drive to work. (4) Park car, spend day at work, get back in car, warning light is no longer on and does not flash or come on at all during the drive home.

(I think I know what you're about to ask. Let's go there.) Just so happens I have a tire pressure gauge in the car. There's a long, wonderful, misty-eyed story about my grandfather behind why it's there. (Another time for that one.) The first few times the light began flashing, I immediately took notice. Found a safe place and pulled over. Grabbed the gauge and checked all four tires. And... they were all close to the mark. Fine. No problems.

Remember the story though? Cold weather always seemed to be involved. And, later in the day, the light was out and did not come back on. Since I checked the tires, and the light went out, I decided there could be something involved in the temperature and time of day and so on that I might be missing. Our mechanic checked the system and found nothing wrong, and I stopped worrying about it.

A few years later—coincidentally within a few hundred miles after the warranty expired (I know... stunning)—the tire pressure light came on and has never gone out. All four tires were fine. All four tires are fine. No pressure problems. No other problems. Everything is both hunky and dory. But now the mechanic is finding a problem with the sensor, which will cost more for repair than I care to reveal. And that is the part driving me bananas.

The issue here isn't whether or not technology is improving things. Overall, sure, it is. And the idea of having lights on my dashboard that can assist me in making small repairs and adjustments for my vehicle that could ultimately avoid major and costly problems down the road... well, that's awesome. It's just not turning out to be the reality.

Instead... lights go on when sensors and such decide an oil change is overdue... lights go on when sensors burn out... lights go on when... hold on, let's summarize this instead of listing all of it...

It both confuses and frustrates me, to extreme levels, that when bells and whistles begin sounding to tell me there's a problem with the car, the most frequent issue is with the bells and whistles and not the car.

Tire pressure? Fine. Warning light? On. Problem? Sensor checking the pressure is broken.

Car? Running great. Smooth and wonderful. Gas mileage never been better. Service engine soon light? On. Problem. Sensor is broken.

The exhaust system is running absolutely perfectly. Emissions levels are fine. But the sensor checking to make sure it's running well is broken. My patience... that's breaking too.

We take care of our vehicles. Oil changes. Repairs.

We have a mechanic we trust, bring repeat business, and recommend to others.

Without launching a massive defense of our automotive habits and peculiarities, simple concept... if a warning light is on, we notice and investigate... if something needs to be done, it gets done.

Which brings us back to the frustrations.

I'm thrilled that my car wants to tell me something is wrong. Brilliant.

I'm not so thrilled that far more often, when these lights go on the vast majority of times the problem is not with what is being monitored but rather with what is monitoring it.

I don't think the car... and, apparently, everyone in the boardroom at the car manufacturer's home office... has a clue about boys screaming wolf. Perhaps, someday, technology in the future will catch up to the sound advice from the past.

Slow and steady saves my life

Having lived in the northeast my entire life, I've learned a thing or two about driving in bad weather... in the ice... in the snow. Of course, this year flipped things around a bit, with snow falling in ridiculous amounts and temperatures plummeting to ridiculous lows, and the snow not necessarily falling where it was expected to fall and thermometers heading to numbers seldom read and never as often in previous years. But one thing remains the same...

Most New Englanders don't know how to drive in bad weather.

Oh, settle down, it's not personal. In fact, most people don't know how to drive in bad weather. It's not exclusive to the New England states. It includes New York. It includes Pennsylvania. New Jersey... Maryland... Delaware... and then start heading west. I can virtually guarantee you the story is the same just about any place you care to mention.

This comes with the understanding, of course, that the larger the state the more open land becomes involved, and the chances of actually hitting something other than a cow or sliding into a drainage ditch go down accordingly. It's one of those size of the state to obstacle in the way inversely proportional ratio kind of things.

This also should not be confused with actually knowing how to drive in bad weather. If you want to seem high comedy, drop an inch of snow on the ground in Texas or Florida and watch the hilarity that follows. They don't know how to do anything in the ice.

The trick is, in many of these places... say, again, Florida... drivers also don't pretend that they know how to operate their vehicles when snow is falling.

As far as I can tell, the primary problem is a complete lack of understanding for the rules of driving in bad weather. People don't respect the rules. People don't take responsibility for following the rules. The rules are simple enough, and there are only four.

> *Rule number one* – Don't touch the brake pedal.

> *Rule number two* – No, really, don't touch the brake pedal.

> *Rule number three* – Keep moving at a consistent speed.

> *Rule number four* – DON'T TOUCH THE BRAKE PEDAL.

The foundation of this lack of understanding problem appears to be a sense of entitlement. In short, a feeling of: "Oh look, I have a license from the great state of (insert name of a New England state here), and therefore I intuitively know how to drive in the snow."

No you don't.

Having a license from a New England state does not automatically bless you with the understanding of whether to turn into the slide or against the slide when you find yourself in one.

Having a license from a New England state does not prevent you from turning your car into an out-of-control sled if you fail to understand what I actually mean by rule number one, rule number two or rule number four.

Having a license from a New England state does not allow you or your vehicle to defy the laws of physics and nature as you think about rule number three and slow down while approaching a hill. (Usually with cars behind you.)

No... being a New Englander doesn't bring with it an ability to handle snow without a thought.

Instead, it brings with it stories of people such as those that trash their trucks in an attempt to become a millionaire. (Wish I was kidding. Here's one story I know of...)

Once I was working with this kid that had decided he was going to quit his job, since the winter was on the way and he had just bought a new truck. Yup, the money was literally going to be overflowing from his checking account once he got the plow blade attached and the flakes began falling. He had his resignation all but signed.

Unfortunately for him, and his truck, until the snow actually fell and the deposits were being made at the bank, he didn't have much money after purchasing it and decided that attaching a plow blade was something he could do on his own. And, to be fair, I was told that he did successfully attach one to his truck. What he didn't do was look into things like the suspension and transmission and... well... you may see the results coming. He *destroyed* his brand new truck. Heck, he did more than that. Since his truck wasn't designed for plowing, and he had elected to attached one of the largest blades available (you know, because of all the plowing jobs he was going to get that would surely include massive parking lots and businesses), he managed to void his warranty.

Of course, much of that didn't matter. Since so many other people had been plowing for years and had established their contacts and contracts, he wasn't finding many in need of his services. Businesses had long since made arrangements for their needs. He was effectively left only with the option of running ads and hoping his phone would ring. And oh yeah... in one of those amazing twists for this story, it turned out that was a mild winter. Which meant once he had finished repairing everything, there wasn't that much plowing to do anyway. The only thing piling up was his bills.

Now... please... understand I am not saying anything negative about people that have snow plows on their trucks. Many of these people have been battling against nature for years, clearing streets and driveways for us so that we may travel more safely. They often are out there for hours, and are called upon around the clock. And they have certainly learned over time, with mistakes providing bills for maintenance and repairs as well as experience.

What I'm being critical of is the people that don't understand the responsibility involved in addressing bad weather, and don't take these things seriously. Let's move off of people plowing the snow and turn to Facebook for a moment.

During some of the storms this winter, especially in Connecticut and Rhode Island, I saw tons of pictures on Facebook. People were posting status updates, and several of them were tweeting away on Twitter as well. There were all sorts of warnings about being slow and careful. There were alerts and notices about accidents and closures and detours.

Incredibly, if you followed the postings, you might have begun to notice something remarkable. It sure as heck seemed like a huge chunk of them were being completed while the person was on the road. Yup... they were in a storm and on roads that were so dangerous that they felt the need to warn everyone about it... and were using a cell phone to take pictures, send text messages, and log on to post things all over the internet. And once they made multiple posts, combining the stories created a timeline... some made it clear that they were likely alone in their car... so they were driving the vehicle. One that I saw actually caught the speedometer on the dashboard registering between 20 and 25... so yeah, I feel comfortable saying they were moving when they snapped the shot.

If you really want to help me out, just keep your car moving along and stop worrying about getting that picture that shows how horrible the driving conditions are. And please, understand why I'm hoping you stay away from your brakes.

~ ~ ~ ~ ~

I should like to point out, that this article should not be viewed in any way as instructional or informative. I absolutely do not mean that you shouldn't use the brake pedal in your car. I did not tell to you turn the wheel into or away from the direction of your sliding vehicle. And there is no way that my suggestion when approaching a hill is to pin the accelerator pedal to the floor.

Instead, just put your cell phone away, stop worrying about telling us how horrible the conditions

are outside at the exact same moment you are driving in those horrible conditions and pay attention.
       Thank you.

The best cookie

What's the best cookie?

I know… I know… there isn't an answer.

There isn't an answer because it isn't a fair question. I might as well be asking about places to live, cars to drive, and—really, going to the extremes —colors.

The best cookie? Trying to pick a winner between green and blue might be an easier debate to settle.

But… humor me… the cookie thing.

In general terms, I feel fairly confident that if someone offered up a homemade, warm from the oven, chocolate chip cookie as the winner, there wouldn't be a parade of villagers carrying torches headed toward the judge's home. There would be disagreements. Depending on the platform for presentation, some might even offer discussions. But… no doubt…

Warm chocolate chip… baked at home… safe choice.

It's more than that though, isn't it? Beyond someone not liking chocolate, wanting pecans, or whatever personal taste or preference might allow one cookie entry into the competition while eliminating another. Warm chocolate chip would be popular. Warm chocolate chip would be—and quite so—safe.

The holidays are what triggered this little debate for me recently. I've actually kicked it around several times before. And it always ends up back to that word... safe. Warm chocolate chip cookies are wonderful... they are also fairly straightforward. Not boring. Not plain. Just not inspiring in such areas as a great cookie debate.

When you start tossing in plans and thoughts and histories for thumbprints and macaroons and cherries and limitless other options, to be served at parties or shared at afternoon swaps, and there is a bit of frost on the windows and the fireplace is glowing and the tree is lit in the corner of the room... cookies get interesting. And few holiday cookie plates will feature chocolate chip cookies as the centerpiece.

Still... I didn't ask about the best holiday cookie. I was wondering about the best cookie. I suppose there are a few ideas that need to be considered.

Number one ~ The generic cookie debate

In this case, we already have our winner. That fresh from the oven, baked with love in our own kitchen, warm chocolate chip. It may be safe. It's also delicious.

Number two ~ The special event cookie

I outlined the holidays, but lots of people make special cookies for a ridiculously wide range of reasons. It could be a summer barbecue as easily as a church bazaar. Plus, there is more than a run of November and December holidays for special events, and this is where I would place any of those extra fancy "grandma's special recipe" types of things where a family tradition comes into consideration.

And, number three ~ The not homemade cookie

It is here that things get really interesting if you want to have a good old-fashioned argument. Because if you're thinking of knocking off a great warm chocolate chip, it seems to me that the way to do it begins with snow on the ground, carolers at the front door, and cookies with coconut and cranberries ready to serve. The right time... the right place... safe and popular may be toppled.

In the aisles of your grocery store, all of the accepted truths and variations are gone. The chocolate chip cookies there aren't the best. Not even close. Some are decent. Some have been around for generations. But no grocery store aisle chocolate chip cookie will ever be voted the best cookie in the world.

And with these classifications produced, we are left with an interesting little scenario developing.

First... In general, I think we would all allow the homemade chocolate chip cookie to be the best cookie in the world. If for no other reason than we can all see that no fairly conducted vote could ever be held where another cookie could win. It might not be a definitive victory... "favorite" and "best" becoming decided by popularity in a place where definitive judgments are simply not possible… and yet it likely wouldn't be close.

Second… For the holiday and special event idea, there can be no winner at all. There are simply too many varieties and differences to consider. Sugar cookies? Gingerbread Men? Bars or biscotti? Meringues? Rum balls? You may never find two voters with the same winner.

No argument one way, and no winner in another. Which brings us to what may be the real debate…

What's the best cookie you can buy? You know… at a store.

I'm going to throw two names out there… Oreos and Lorna Doones.

Oreos… yeah… simple and likely not too much of a surprise. In their own way, safe. I can't provide any statistical data or even personal efforts of questioning people, but I think the Oreo is effectively the store-bought cookie version of the home baked chocolate chip… all purpose and unapproachable. If you want to open a debate such as chocolate chip cookies with and without nuts while still allowing it to be the top cookie either way, fine, we can debate the classic and Double Stuf Oreos. I do believe that overall Oreos are the cookies racking up the most sales each year.

So, you likely understand an Oreo being suggested. But a shortbread cookie?

Yeah… I said it… a shortbread cookie.

I bring up Lorna Doone as a second nomination from me for two reasons. First, it is an awesome cookie. And second, there happen to be some people—and I mention this in fairness to them even though I do believe such individuals should be approached with caution—that claim they don't like chocolate. A Lorna Doone has a solid following and is readily available. A Lorna Doone is worthy of note.

And even here, selecting a winner comes with problems.

Over the next few weeks, I will be sending texts to my mother, looking for recipes in family archives and personal books, and considering all sorts of seasonal favorites. I'll be dreaming of pecan tarts, searching for peanut butter cookies with a Hershey's Kiss on top, and trying to decide if I want to buy some of the ingredients I'll need (but only use) for some terrific seasonal delights.

It's Christmas... and that means some incredible baking opportunities. And it's enough to occasionally make me wonder... are homemade chocolate chip and Oreo cookies truly the best?

You may agree with some of this. You may disagree. If you have another contender though, please feel free to let me know. (And, if you could, include a recipe with your message. Just so we can perform truly thorough research.)

A snowstorm and a chainsaw... not exactly the first thought in my head

A friend of mine posted on Facebook the other day. Post made me laugh... then it made me think.

The laughter part was the first reaction, and reading it still makes me chuckle. Snow was falling, and had reached roughly a foot in height already.

(It's here in our story that I should point out she posted this in September. And probably should add that she lives in Alaska. Back to the story...)

The kids were home because of the snow... the snow was continuing to fall... and a tree was blocking the driveway.

Hey... ha ha... life in beautiful Alaska. It might seem like a cold winter is ramping up for the northeast... and maybe the leaves had begun turning a bit early before holding off for what appears to be a beautiful and timely oncoming October foliage... but, yeah, we're not wading through a foot-plus of snow to pick apples.

I commented on the post, made fun of her a bit while exchanging some comments, and moved along.

That's when the chainsaw that had been rattling around came to the forefront and connected with something.

See... I have a chainsaw. Used it a few times. I've felled trees. (Felled. That's a strange word. Who the heck came up with that? Fall... fallen... falls... felled? I'm not even sure if I'm using it properly. Especially since even though autocorrect seems to agree with it, that's hardly a ringing and trustworthy endorsement of proper grammar or use. (Use? Usage?) Anyway...) I've cut down a few trees. Cleared some parts of the yard. Worked on a pile of logs to make firewood and all sorts of lovely projects.

At this point in my life though, I've never had to use a chainsaw on something across my driveway. In the yard... yes. Seen trees take down power lines and block roads, all fortunately not at my home... sure. But I cannot recall a tree that had fallen in such a way, was in my yard, and was large enough that I needed to break out the chainsaw to clear the driveway.

Amazingly though, we need to go back to her post. Remember... not only was a tree blocking her driveway, it was also spotted around sunrise after one of those majestic, beautiful, perfectly normal and likely everyday Alaskan overnight drops of a foot of snow. My first impulse? I had commented on the snow and the kids being around.

I'm guessing that if you've been around snow a few times in your life, you've probably encountered those lovely mornings of inconvenience. And if you happen to be of working age, and not just young enough that you are waking up and hoping upon hope that school will be cancelled so you can go outside and try to build a fort out of fluffy snow that won't stick together, you may have debated the use of a weather-related call out as opposed to waking up extra early to shovel.

Ok... so work is at 9am... takes an hour to get there, especially since the roads may be a bit iffy after the storm... and then there's a shower, breakfast, taking care of the dogs, and... normally the alarm goes off around 7.

Need to shovel the driveway? Break out the snow blower? (Ahh... excuse me... snow *thrower*. Who came up with that one? Does anyone actually say snow thrower? That's got to be worse than remembering whether or not you felled a tree. Doesn't matter right now, you still need to get up at least an extra hour ahead of usual to clean off the car.)

There you are, in a warm bed, figuring there won't be much traffic on the road since most normal people called out and slept in, and you could probably pick up enough speed so that after clearing just enough off the windshield you could navigate onto the road and then be able to pick up speed to get the rest of the snow blown off the car.

(Full disclosure... I completely clear off our cars before hitting the road. Even the roofs. I am taking some literary freedoms for fun. Ok? We all know people that don't clean off the entire car, and the bed was really, really toasty.)

Suffice to say that even after possibly creating another twenty minutes of sleep with your windshield decision on a morning when you began by losing an hour of it, up there in Alaska my friend added a tree across the driveway to the troubles. (And she just kind of casually added it in.)

Blocking the driveway? Probably not a branch or a skinny little thing. Probably a project.

Honestly, firing up the snow blower is one thing. If I had to break out the chainsaw and wade through a mountain of snow to get to a tree, cut that tree, and clear it away before I could even really use the snow blower... well... I'd likely give up and hope we had enough food to make it to the spring thaw.

All of which is a nice way of understanding why I can watch a show like *Mountain Men*, think about how beautiful it would be to build a cabin on my own and stay there for a bit, and never, ever, actually do it.

Because there are limits... and trudging through a foot of snow with a chainsaw is on the far side of the line in the concept of things I'd do to get to work.

That falling snow is beautiful. (Especially when viewed through a window, sitting in a chair with a blanket covering you, with a warm mug in your hands.)

Sunset

How often have you watched a sunset? Or, even a sunrise?

I've been fortunate in my life. I've been able to experience such moments in all sorts of tremendous locations. Sunsets for instance…

One evening I pulled the car into a rest area along the Kancamagus Highway in New Hampshire. A group of friends was with me, and we got out and enjoyed a beautiful sunset.

Spent a brilliant day with family in the Joshua Tree National Park. We ended our visit by driving out to the Keys View location for the sunset.

Began a day with a stop at the Hoover Dam, cruised along Route 66, and then ended the drive with a sunset at the Grand Canyon.

I've been in Key West—including Mallory Square and on a sailboat—for multiple sunsets.

And lately, our home is situated perfectly for me to see the sunrise over a field off one side of our yard and the sunset in the distance of another.

Those are just a few moments. And I would trade none of them.

Part of those memories are times spent with friends and family. Investments and benefits of relationships. I could attempt to return, but they could never be repeated. They are our experiences... my experiences... and the value cannot be accurately measured in any way beyond concepts such as love and smiles.

When I began this book, I scratched the surface of what it means to have a parkside view. It's that seat for observation. A bench, in the park, where you can watch the activity around you. And the theme I danced around was one of being able to appreciate what is taking place without being just a spectator. The reality though, is that it is so much more.

People use sunrises and sunsets for many different purposes. Some of them are literal. Several are figurative. The passage of time. Endings and beginnings. Markers along the way. Metaphors for life.

For many years, Terry and I lived in a house surrounded by towering oaks. Dozens of them. In fact, I'm sure, hundreds of them. Thick and glorious and deep. We wanted to have a garden, and actually did, though we struggled to find the perfect location as direct sunlight was limited. Those oaks made sure that sun was blocked for many of the morning hours and cut off by mid-afternoon.

(That's the literal of it. Figuratively speaking...)

There are times in all of our lives when things are distorted, blocked, and impossible to see completely. Obligations and realities get in the way of pausing and appreciating. Not pausing and appreciating anything specific... just being able to pause and appreciate whatever.

That's only a shame when we let it become the norm and fail to grab the opportunity to observe a few special moments along the journey.

My intention with this essay was never to be overly sappy or amazingly heavy-handed in pushing the idea of appreciation for the truly majestic moments. You can make plans and designs, with them often coming to fruition. You don't need me to create new ways of expressing old clichés. Instead...

At several moments in your life, you'll be out on the road. There'll be a rest area coming up, and you'll have the chance to pull over. I hope that occasionally you will. Perhaps take the time to enjoy a picnic with friends... maybe just sit still and watch the sunset. Such opportunities do indeed happen every day. But we don't always have the ability to enjoy them when they do.

About the Author

Around the time Bob was six-years-old, his parents attended a meeting with his teacher. She explained to them that of all the children she had ever taught, "Little Bobby" was the one she would most want to be marooned on an island with because of his amazing stories. This did not shock his parents.

Since that time, Bob has managed to avoid being stranded—alone or in a group—on a deserted island. However, he has: graduated from Syracuse University, been an instructor for several Red Cross courses, worked at the largest casino in the world, and in all sorts of wonderful ways repeatedly avoided utilizing his English degree and medical background.

He's also been sharing his stories.

In March of 2003, Bob brought his writing efforts to the internet with his own web site, *In My Backpack*. (www.inmybackpack.com) Since the earliest of its posts, the site has included general interest essays, sports and travel material, and captured the flavors-of-the-day with an on-going journal entry area. He has conducted hundreds of interviews, many of which have appeared on his site and in his books.

Though Bob has always considered himself more of "a writer with a camera", that hasn't stopped him from creating a sizeable portfolio. On his web site, photo galleries exist for several entertainers, as well as a feature on the award-winning exhibition *Diana: A Celebration*. His photography efforts have been used by groups such as *Legends in Concert* and Foxwoods Resort Casino, and have also appeared in several print and on-line outlets.

Born and raised in Rhode Island, and a Connecticut resident for almost two decades, Bob currently lives in New York with his wife, Terry.

The 'ville

The *In My Backpack* web site has grown just a bit since the early days back in 2003.

The site was originally intended to be s testing ground of sorts... a place where Bob could post his writing, shake off some rust, float a few trial balloons, and so on. Experiments and fun.

It became a bit more as interviews and photo galleries joined the party. Then, in 2012, the publication of *Time Just Drifts Away* added to the equation.

Today the web site is actually more of a family of sites. Part of the offerings now are ComplemenTerry Designs and Local Friends for Local Business. Bob's writing has continued to expand, such as with the inclusion of the newsletter that provided the material for this collection, *A Parkside View*.

Most of these projects have pages on social media sites as well. There, you can find special announcements, details about upcoming events, and more. And we would be grateful if you would check some of these pages out (and follow and like them).

Bob's Writing

On Facebook
In My Backpack
Time Just Drifts Away

On Twitter
@bobinmybackpack

ComplemenTerry Designs

On Facebook
CT Designs

On Twitter
@cterrydesigns

Local Friends for Local Business

On Facebook
Local Friends for Local Business

On Twitter
@friendslocal

*** Some web sites and social media pages use similar names. Please contact us if you have any questions ***

67769995R00108

Made in the USA
Middletown, DE
25 March 2018